10/13

Soldiering –

Yesterday

from boyhood to manhood
Oct 14, 1942 - Oct 28, 1945

by

Roger H. Aldrich

ACKNOWLEDGEMENTS

The photos on pages 13, 22, 23, 35 and 38 are from the national archives. All of the other photos and drawings are from my own collection.

Everett Rowley of Sherwin Dodge has been of immense help to me. I think I must have missed school on the day they taught punctuation, but "Rett" rescued me. I am also very appreciative of his supportive comments.

Nancy has always been able to lift me out of my black moods - and there were a lot of them as I moved back through time to write this book. She is my wife, my lover, my very understanding audience and my best friend.

It is nearly impossible for me to express my gratitude to my friend Dr. Kadimah Michelson. "Kim" has a way of inspiring me to reach beyond my grasp. Through my writing she sees into my soul as no other person has ever done.

ISBN Number 0-9702899-0-1
Copyright 1995
First Printing May, 1995
Second Printing July, 2000
Roger H. Aldrich
Hildex Farm
672 State Hwy. 117
Sugar Hill, NH 03585-4227

Composition was done with Word 6
on a PC by Roger Aldrich

Printed at
Sherwin Dodge Printers
Littleton, NH, USA

This book is dedicated to
all of those young men who never came home.
They haunted me for years but now
I am at peace with them.

1939 - At Home on the Farm

From left to right: Dr. Emerson, Homer Aldrich, Dorothy Aldrich, Mrs. Emerson, Gramp Berry, Roger Aldrich. In back, Robert Emerson and Mary Emerson. The photo was taken by Margaret, Mary's sister, out by the barn at the "Red Cottage" on Mr. Henry H. Crapo's "Cooley Farm," Sugar Hill, NH.

We first became acquainted with the Emerson sisters, Mary and Margaret when they came to our home which was part of the American Youth Hostel system. Mary spent a number of summers with us while she was a student at Cornell University where her father was a professor. Mary was my "big sister" while I was going to high school. She was a kind, gentle and extremely intelligent person - great fun to be with. I wish Mary could have read this book. She died on my birthday, 31 March, 1994.

iv

FORWARD

I have been writing this book for a very long time. Fifty years to be exact, but I have never put anything on paper until now. You may rightly wonder why I have bothered to do it at all at this late date. Up to 1994 the story had all been in my mind. Some of the incidents that I tell about have been told, repeatedly, to friends and family. They always listen politely, but with glazed-over eyes. I remember listening to war stories told by veteran acquaintences and wishing that they would write them down, so I could remember them. I have been a history buff since I was a small child and have read military history over the years to such an extent that I have become a somewhat better than average military historian. I have read untold numbers of personal historys, but they seldom reveal the inner feelings of the writer. In this narrative I have tried to give the readers (particularly my friends and my decendants) an insight to my thoughts as I experienced World War II. Now that I have written this all down, I won't have to tell it again; my oral history has been "chiseled in stone." There are, however, quite a few new stories that have not been told before, for I could never bear to put them into words. There are some long repressed memories here that I have finally unchained. While freeing the memories I have freed myself.

This narrative is as true and factual as I can make it. All of the things that I have written about, actually happened. My Mother saved all of my letters and I relied heavily on them to bolster my memory. The 62nd Engineer Co. Assn. has had an annual reunion for many years and, while I have never been able to attend, they kindly keep me posted and have made available many interesting items of the Company's history. I know, for instance, exactly where we were bivouacked each night from the time I joined the company to the time it was disbanded.

I started writing with a computer/word processor some years ago and frequently get the feeling that my thoughts are flowing from my mind directly to the screen in front of me. While writing this story I found things appearing on the screen that I had not remembered for years and years. What a marvelous thing the mind is --- it retains events that we thought we had "deleted." Suppressed memories remain locked away in some small storage compartment of the mind's attic and when the proper key is turned in the lock, there they are, waiting to be looked at again.

If any of the former members of the 62nd or their relatives should happen to read this narrative, they may not remember things the same as I do. We do not all see the same things at the same time so why should one person's memories be the same as another person's? In "The Birth of Britain," Vol. One of "A History of the English-Speaking Peoples," Sir Winston Churchill (my hero), while discussing the legends of King Arthur, says, "The reserve of modern assertions is sometimes pushed to extremes, in which the fear of being contradicted leads the writer to strip himself of almost all sense and meaning."

Churchill goes on to say, "....It is all true, or it ought to be; ...." I'm sure he would say the same about the story you are about to read.

Psalms 139,Verse 9

If I take the wings of the morning,
and dwell in the uttermost parts
of the sea,
even there thy hand shall lead me,
and thy right hand shall hold me.

Alpha --- Fort Leonard Wood, Mo.

Survival is something everyone has to learn one way or another. Some do a better job at it than others. When I went on active duty in the Army in February, 1943, I had to learn quickly how to survive in the military and learning that simple lesson helped me to survive, literally, when I got to where the shooting was going on. After induction at Fort Devens, Massachusetts, I was sent to Fort Leonard Wood, Missouri, to do my basic training, since I had enlisted in the Engineer Corp, much to the disgust of the people who processed my papers. They thought I should go into the Air Corp or Artillery since I had a choice, being a volunteer, but I insisted on the Engineers. I was studying Civil Engineering at Northeastern University in Boston when the war broke out in 1941. I had volunteered for the Enlisted Reserve Corp. on Oct. 14, 1942 and found that my grades were slipping badly as the country got deeper into the war. My Co-op job through the University was with the United States Coast and Geodetic Survey and as my ten-week period came to an end in Jackson, Miss., in January of '43 I made up my mind to request active duty, which is how I wound up in Fort Devens in February. At Fort Leonard Wood I learned a lot of important things like, how to blouse my trouser legs down over my canvas leggings, (so as not to look like a Billy Goat, as one Sgt. put it), how to properly salute an officer, how to wash my mess utensils so that I wouldn't get dysentery. I learned how to sing "Deep in the Heart of Texas," at the PX in order not to get beaten up by the Texas guys who hung out there and demanded that song from everyone who didn't have a southern accent. I learned how to shoot a paper target silhouette in the heart from 200 yards and how to bayonet a straw filled dummy so that he wouldn't fight back . I learned how to wear a gas mask and run a mile or so while that cursed thing restricted my breathing. I learned how to climb ropes like a monkey and how to build bridges and how to paddle a pontoon and how to drive a bulldozer and how to set up tents and how to sleep in one in a pouring rain. But the thing I liked best was learning how to use explosives. Wow! I was getting paid fifty

3

dollars a month with my board and room thrown in to have 4th-of-July fun every day. We were taught how to use dynamite and TNT and black powder and Plastique, which we called composition C, and primer cord and blasting caps and fuses and electric exploders and mines and hand grenades and all sorts of good stuff like that, the knowledge of which has served me well ever since, because the most important thing I learned about explosives was don't get near the damned things if you can help it.

The training platoon to which I was assigned was made up, almost entirely, of college age guys like myself. We were all unhappy with Hitler for interrupting our education but our high spirits had by no means been interrupted. We were extremely ill mannered to our sergeants and kept them in a constant state of nervousness, wondering what kind of malicious mischief we would come up with next, hoping that whatever it was would not come to the notice of any of the officers. The more the sergeants yelled and screamed at us, the more pranks we played on them. Our bunk room was on the second level of the barracks and the sergeants had quarters on the ground floor. One night we were "raising the roof" after lights-out and our sergeant threatened us with a "hike" if he heard "One more peep outa you guys." He made it to the bottom of the stairs when someone yelled, "PEEP." So the sergeant, having made the threat, now had to produce and we all got up, got dressed and went outside to do close-order drill in the dark for half an hour. We went back inside, and stood at attention while the sergeant lectured us on military discipline, after which we got undressed and back in our bunks. The sergeant, satisfied that we had learned our lesson, turned out the lights and went down the stairs. As soon as his boots hit the first floor he was serenaded by a chorus of "PEEPS" from above. Up we got again and out we went to march again for an hour. This time when we got back upstairs, the sergeant made a monstrous mistake. He said, "If I hear anymore out of you people we will go for a five mile hike with helmets, gas masks, full field packs and weapons." He made it to the first floor again when someone yelled out, "Do you want the weapons loaded sergeant?" We were marching briskly along about two miles into

4

the hike when a deep voice in the rear commanded, "Column right, March" and we all headed down the street where "Officer's Row" was located. While the fuming sergeant was trying to find out who had given the command, the deep voice again boomed out, "Double-time, March" and we all started running down the street like a herd of wild elephants. To add to the hilarity the voice again commanded us, "Count cadence, Count." And the thundering herd all went roaring down the street, shouting in unison, "Hup, two three, four - Hup, two three four." Lights started coming on in the officer's houses on both sides of the street as we passed by and we hadn't gone much further when we were met by a jeep carrying three MPs who soon had us halted and headed back toward our barracks. They tried to march us quietly but it is an impossibility to march a hundred men in boots quietly on a paved street, and it is especially so when they start singing, loudly, "I don't wanna go to war no more. Gee, ma, I wanna go—gee, ma, I wanna go—gee, ma, I wanna go home.". When we arrived back at the barracks we were met by our unhappy platoon Lieutenant. He didn't make the mistake of threatening us with a hike, instead he revoked our PX privileges for a week and promised us more if we didn't act like soldiers instead of high-school students. He didn't need to be so serious and severe; we were all ready for some sleep by then anyway, as dawn was just breaking. Apparently the powers above decided that the affair had been more the sergeant's fault than ours, as he was the one who lost control of us. All of the platoon sergeants and the officers were very careful never to mention the incident again in our presence. I did hear by the grape-vine that the sergeant involved was being reassigned to a combat unit and that there had been a great deal of hilarity in the Officers' Club about the way our platoon had awakened the senior officers and had outsmarted that unpopular sergeant.

As our training drew to a close, I found that I had scored high enough so that I was given a choice of going to Officers Candidate School or to the Army Specialized Training Program. The ASTP was designed to send promising students to various colleges where we were supposed to get a degree in some militarily related field in

5

two to three years of accelerated study. At the end of our study and graduation we were promised automatic promotion to Second Lieutenant. This sounded like a golden opportunity to finish my education and honorably escape combat so I chose that road rather than OCS. That choice probably saved my life, for had I gone to OCS and become a 2nd Lieutenant, I would certainly have wound up in a Combat Engineer company. I was sent from Fort Leonard Wood to the University of Nebraska where I was assigned to Carnegie Tech. in Pittsburgh, Pa. Things went well at Carnegie and I did well enough in my studies to be promoted from Private to Private First Class. About July or August my grades started slipping drastically and I began to realize that I was not going to be able to keep up with the accelerated program. I got out voluntarily in September of 1943, and soon thereafter the Army decided that either the war wasn't going to last all that long or they needed more fighting manpower and ASTP was dismantled and all of the students, all over the country, were pulled out of academicia and dumped into replacement depots, to be sent to the various war theaters as soon as possible. I found myself in Fort Belvoir, Virginia, assigned , like a third wheel on a bicycle, to a Combat Engineer training unit. I had nothing to do except help out the Supply Sergeant and listen to the radio in the company recreation hall as I was exempt from training for I had already done that. For two eventful weeks in November I went on maneuvers with the company up into the Blue Ridge mountains and shivered in a tent, keeping the tools oiled, while the rest of the troops wallowed around in the deep snow playing like engineers, making roads and building bridges. I had a week long furlough home. The time passed in a blur and the only thing that sticks in my memory was the sight of my Dad weeping as I boarded the train in Woodsville to go back to Fort Belvoir. He told Mom that he was never going to see me alive again.

In December I spent a great many useless days on troop trains and in various replacement depots—Virginia to Ohio to Pennsylvania—to wind up at Camp Edwards on Cape Cod, in Massachusetts. I was in a very large group of Engineer replacements, so large in fact, that we were only fed two meals per day. We got in a mile-long chow-line in the morning and after finally getting to eat we went back to the end of the line and shuffled into the late afternoon to have another meal before going to bed.

Just before Christmas, 1943, we were ordered to pack everything in our barracks bags and to send home everything we couldn't carry with us. We were told that if we wanted to call home to do it the next day, but to say nothing about moving. I waited in a long, long line in the December cold, in front of the telephone booths. My feet were practically frozen and even tucked deep into my overcoat I couldn't help shivering. I'm sure that some of my shivering was a result of thoughts of the future. Did I have a future? This was the second Christmas in a row that I had spent with strangers in a strange and lonely place. I was literally rubbing shoulders with thousands of people, yet I was alone, so utterly alone. Now I wanted to reach out and touch Mama. I wanted her to hold me and keep me safe as she had when I was a child, but I couldn't let her feel my fright, I had to bluff it out as I had done so many other times in this past year. Finally it was my turn and I got to call home and talk to Mama. I couldn't think of anything else to say, so I said, "I called to say Merry Christmas, Mom. I love you and Dad and little sister Nancy very, very much. Sorry I can't be with you." In a quavering voice Mama wished me a Merry Christmas too, and asked me if I was on the way overseas. I tried desperately not to choke up for I didn't want her to knew how scared I was—she couldn't see the tears streaming down my face. I said, "Good-bye, Mom. I'll write real soon."

As I walked back to the barracks I thought of Christmases past—of the Christmas Tree in the corner of our cozy living room with the presents, gaily wrapped, piled under the tree. I thought of my little sister, Nancy, two years old, with whom I had yet to spend a Christmas. I thought of going over to Grammy Aldrich's house for Christmas dinner, with all of the family gathered together. There would be Grammy, of course, and Aunt Beat and Uncle

Archie and cousins Bob and Homer and Donnie. There would be
Aunt Helen and Uncle Andrew and cousins Betty and Jean. There
might be cousin Eleanor or maybe Aunt Ella and cousin Bennie.
And there would be Dad and Mama and sister Nancy and Gramp
Berry, who would tell his favorite story about Christmas when he
was very young.

This 1944 Christmas Card was designed by
Henry J. MacMillan of the 62nd Engr. Co.

Atlantic Crossing

We left Camp Edwards the next day or the day after, the shades were pulled on the railroad cars, whether to keep us from seeing where we were going or to keep spies from looking in at us, I do not know. When we dismounted from the train, we could tell by the skyline that we were in Boston. We were hurried up one of the gang-ways and down into the bowels of a troop ship. The ship was a large, former British ocean liner, I have forgotten the name. It was manned by the British Merchant Marine. My assigned bunk space was on the lowest deck in one of the former cargo holds. The bunks were stacked six to eight high with so little space between them that it was impossible to roll over. To change position from one's back to one's stomach it was necessary to get out of the bunk and get back in again. There was so little room between rows of bunks that two people could not pass each other. Needless to say, these crowded living conditions had a rather drastic effect on my phobia, which had developed over the last couple of years. The phobia manifested itself as a fear of confined places or situations and could (and had), lead to panic, if I could not control it. I had acquired the ability to drop off to sleep anywhere, anytime and found that this was the best way to control my phobia—get in my bunk and sleep. I slept my way across the Atlantic. I ate little, for I couldn't stand the food—greasy mutton and very ancient potatoes, boiled to death; carrots that had died long, long ago and some kind of gray bread, made with sawdust and mill sweepings. There was no coffee but some kind of brown beverage, called "Char" by the Brits, but we suspected that it was drainings from a horse barn. I didn't realize at the time that we were being served the same food that the British people had been eating for all the war years. I spent as much time as I could out on the deck watching the other ships in the very large convoy. There were other troop ships, many cargo carriers and several oil tankers. There were destroyers, destroyer-escorts and even one small aircraft carrier, although I doubted that the aircraft, clearly visible on its flight-deck, could take off in the atrocious weather. The rougher it got, and the steeper the seas became, the better I liked it, and I would have spent twenty four hours on deck but the MPs wouldn't allow it, for we were forbidden on deck after dusk. The odor below decks was awesome, what with two or three thousand men seasick and most of them with dysentery also, due to the bad food. I survived by sleeping, while forced to be below, and spending all the time I could out on the weather deck during daylight hours.

Our first "Abandon Ship" drill was a claustrophobic's nightmare come true. The water-tight doors clanged shut and I watched the two or three hundred men in the compartment try to fight, club, claw and kick their way up a single-file ladder leading to a round man-hole-like hatch in the overhead. I said to myself, "The hell with it. I'd rather drown," and I got back into my bunk and went to sleep. I didn't really fancy swimming in the North Atlantic at New Year's time anyway. I never did get out during that drill. All drills after that were enforced by MPs with drawn pistols and everyone went up the ladders in an orderly fashion. We were most of two weeks crossing and landed at Liverpool in the inevitable rain. My branch of the Aldrich family had returned to England three hundred and fourteen years after leaving. And a Happy New Year to you too, Roger.

England

Springtime in England in 1944 was a pleasant change for us soldiers after the dreary winter on Salisbury Plain. We had only had snow once and that only a couple of inches which lasted for a day or two. Mostly it just rained and in the springtime it still rained and we still had some of the cold, raw, windy and cloudy weather that had been with us all winter, but for the most part the weather was warm and delightful. Shortly after I arrived in Britain I had been assigned to the 62nd Engineer Co. (Topo.). The 62nd was a topographic company and did surveying and map making. When in the field we worked closely with the artillery to insure the accuracy of their map coordinates. The company was small with only about 110 men and all of them had been in the African invasion and then the Sicilian invasion. Some few men had gone on to Italy in that invasion, to prepare the way for the rest of the company, but the upper level planners had a change of heart and

10

sent the company to England to train for the European show which everyone, including the Germans, knew was coming sometime in the spring or summer. There were four of us replacements sent to take the place of four men who had been transferred to a Topo Engineer Battalion. We four, Les McCarthy, Bill Pierce, Phil Weiss and myself, had all been on the same troop ship.

Roger and Les McCarthy in front of Hut 47, "Home" at Upton Lovel, Salisbury Plain, England.

Lt. Wilkinson met at the nearest railroad station, took one look at us and said, "Katy, bar the door." I gathered from that remark that we didn't look as if we met his qualifications for fine, outstanding soldiers. We probably were a bedraggled looking group, what with being shuffled from replacement depot to replacement depot and having just gotten off a troop ship. Most of the other men in the company had been in the army since some time in 1942 and some of them were first-draft men who had been taken into the army in 1941, before Pearl Harbor. There were two or three old, grizzled Master Sergeants who were Regular Army and had been about ready to retire when the war came along. The rest of the Company, except for me, were all draftees. I, of coarse, was different, for I had joined the Enlisted Reserve at Northeastern University in October of 1942 and had gone on active duty in February, 1943. By the winter of 1944 most of the people in the Company, except for a few Sad Sacks, had attained a rank higher than PFC, so unless someone was killed or died or drastically misbehaved (all of which was highly unlikely) there was no chance of my advancing in rank before the end of the war. The army had some strange customs, some of which I never did understand the logic of—probably because there wasn't any. On payday, for instance we lined up in order of rank, alphabetically and then by classification. I could understand the ranking order and, of course the alphabetical part, but the classification made no sense at all. The draftees, whose serial numbers started with "3" came first, then Volunteers, whose serial numbers started with "1", (I was the only one), then Regular Army. So I was always last in line except for the three old Master Sergeants. One of the Master Sergeants took a liking to me and took me as his carpenter assistant. I was unhappy at that for I wanted to be out in the field with the surveyors. He was manufacturing some portable, collapsible toilets that were to sit over a hole dug wherever our camp site might be to form our latrines. He was making a six-holer for the enlisted men and a two-holer for the officers. I came to the conclusion that this guy had become a master sergeant by longevity alone and not knowing what else to do with him, the officers had put him in charge of fussing around, i.e., carpenter work, mending tents, counting buttons, etc. The work did not impress me as essential to the war effort and I ducked it as soon as possible by deliberately making mistakes so many times that he finally said to me, "Get out of here. You wouldn't make a pimple on a good carpenter's ass."

A training unit at Stonehenge

I went back to the survey group and we spent the winter surveying Salisbury Plain over and over again. Much to our officers astonishment, we found that Stonehenge was pretty much in the same place and didn't seem to move more than a foot or two each time we surveyed it. We marched a lot, sometimes accompanied by marching songs, usually ribald, for the benefit of the villagers. Our training included weapons training and we were issued new carbines to take the place of the infantry Garrands that we had before. The carbine was light and a much better defensive weapon for non-combat troops, although my particular weapon was so inaccurate that I couldn't guarantee to hit anything at a range of more than one hundred feet.. On Saturday afternoons the company ran trucks to Bath, Bristol or Salisbury, but I had never learned how to dance and there was nothing else to do but drink warm beer in the pubs and I wasn't much for that, so I spent a lot of time reading everything I could get my hands on. In March, I had a three-day pass to London and met an old family friend, Mary Emerson, who was a lieutenant in the WAC's. We went to St. Paul's Cathedral, Westminster Abbey, Buckingham Palace and some of the museums that happened to be open. Once we were stopped by MPs and told that we couldn't walk together for that violated the army regulation which forbade fraternization between officers and enlisted personnel. When they were out of sight we walked together again. Mary was four years my senior and, sometimes with her sister, Margaret, had lived with us off and on in the years when she was in college. I always thought of her as my older sister. We had first met when she came to our place as a Youth Hosteler.

Roger on Salisbury Plain, Winter of 1944

14

Despite the dreary weather, we managed to have some comfort from a pot bellied, coal-burning stove in our Quonset hut barracks. Sometime in May the logistics of the invasion plan caught up with us and we were moved out of our warm huts and into tents at a camp site closer to the coast. The new camp was a virtual prison camp, surrounded by barbed wire and guards, who were posted to keep us in as much as to keep prying eyes out. When we moved into this camp our training stopped. Those few of us below the rank of corporal were formed into a permanent guard and there was a twenty-four hour guard on a small perimeter around our press trucks. The presses were kept running around the clock printing, we knew not what. From the size of the paper going in, and the full crates coming out, we assumed that they were printing large maps. And since we had been quarantined with much secrecy, we expected that the maps were invasion maps. This would explain the tight security, tighter in fact, than any of our neighboring troops, with whom we were allowed no contact. While we were allowed to receive mail, we were not allowed to send any and we learned later that all of us had relatives who were frantic because we had all seemed to disappear. Life became an endless round of four hours on guard duty and four hours off, four hours on again and another four hours off. One day blended into the next and we became incapable of telling where we were on the calendar or what time it was other than by distinguishing between night (it became dark) or day (it became light). Sleep. I craved sleep more than any other thing in the world. It was impossible to get enough sleep in the four hours allotted to us and we became automated zombies, plodding around and around those cursed press trucks for four hours then crawling into our pup tents for as much sleep as we could get, resenting the time necessary to eat and attend to bodily functions to say nothing of inspections, company formations, shaving and brushing our teeth. For all that, we were better off than the pressmen for they had to work sixteen hours on and eight hours off.

There were others in the company detailed to the regular guard around the company perimeter whose schedule was the normal four hours on and eight hours off for a 24 hour period. Those of us on press truck security had special orders. Our carbines were always to be loaded with one round in the chamber and the safety on. No one, other than the two pressmen, were allowed inside the guard perimeter unless accompanied by Captain Kent. This order, we were told, included even the company lieutenants. We were further ordered to shoot anyone trying to gain access to the press trucks after disobeying our order to halt. This was pretty serious stuff. Could I really shoot anyone in American uniform if he refused to stop? I truly didn't know, but I was about to find out. On one of my morning shifts a full Colonel, resplendent with a silver Eagle perched on each shoulder, approached. I halted him and informed him that he would have to go to the company office and would have to be accompanied by Capt. Kent to enter the press trucks. The Colonel told me, very forcefully, that he was Colonel So-and-so of 19th Corp headquarters and he had access to anything and anywhere that he wanted to go and no Private First Class was going to tell him otherwise and he made a move toward the steps of the press truck. I took the safety off my carbine, changed from a port arms position to pointing the carbine at his chest and said, "Sir, I have taken the safety off and if you do not stop, I will shoot you." I laid particular emphasis on the word "will." I could hear my voice trembling as, I assume, could he. He said, "You are facing a court-martial." I said, "Sir, I am carrying out my orders." He turned and headed toward the company office tent and soon could be seen coming back with Capt. Kent. I expected, like Chicken Little, that the Sky, or something equally unpleasant, was about to fall on me. The Colonel said, "Soldier, this company has just passed a very serious security check, thanks to you for sticking to your orders. I congratulate you." I thought I was going to faint and could think of nothing to say so I brought my carbine up to the present arms position and the Colonel and Capt. Kent went into the press truck after returning my salute. I had been in the army for fifteen months and at last I felt that I was a real soldier.

Crossing the Channel

We knew that D-Day had arrived because all of the Combat Engineer outfits around us had pulled out the day before and the number of planes going over was just incredible. We saw a flight of British fighters that we didn't recognize; I thought they were some kind of Spitfire but someone else said no, they were Hurricanes. We were both wrong for they were Typhoons, a relatively new Brit. tank buster. We didn't know any more about what was going on than the people on the home front did, our only news was Armed Forces Radio, Axis Sally and the BBC. Our presses stopped printing about D-7 and we got a look at the maps of Normandy that our pressmen had been churning out. Our platoon lieutenant said to look at them good for our camp site was all picked out and we would be going in another week. The motor pool guys spent all their time water-proofing our vehicle engines and fitting them with long air-breathing snorkel tubes and high exhaust pipes so that the vehicles could get off our LST into six or seven feet of water if necessary. So on D-13 we struck our tents, loaded our trucks and headed down to Southampton. We spent all day helping the drivers back their vehicles onto LST 383. The ship was manned by the US. Coast Guard and the sailors kidded us unmercifully. The told us that LST meant Large Slow Target and they hoped we all knew how to swim We started across the Channel before dawn on June 19 with the seas getting steeper and steeper and no let-up in the rain and low flying, ragged clouds. By the time the coast of Normandy came into view the ship was rising and plunging dramatically There was a monstrous following sea and first the stern would rise, rise, rise until the wave slid down the side and the ship would be on an even keel for a moment and then the stern would start to fall off into the trough as the bow rose higher and higher and higher until the sea fell away from it and down it would plunge again I always had, and still have to this day, an apparent immunity to sea-sickness, but most of the rest of the company were so sick they didn't care if the ship sank or not. I had been enjoying the sea and the rough weather out on deck all the time since we left England but our Lieutenant informed me that I'd better pick a bunk below as we were going to have to anchor off the beach because conditions were too rough to land. There was a round, water-tight hatch in the deck that led to our narrow compartment below with the bunks stacked three high as on a troop-ship. I took one look and could feel my claustrophobic panic rising and decided that I would sleep on the barracks bags in the truck that was my assigned riding place. My Brooklyn-Irish tent mate decided to join me under the canvas bow-covering of the truck. The barracks bags made a softer bed than we would have had down below anyway. The guys in the platoon had arranged for me to be Nolan's bunkmate when I first came to the company. Nobody liked him and he snored loudly but compared to my grandfather's, Nolan's snores were mild. Gramp sounded like a thunderstorm compared to Nolan's mild rumble. Nolan was eccentric, to say the least, and I was the only person who had been able to get along with him since the company left the States, so most of the guys were grateful to me for taking him off their backs. He was obviously a loner, as was I, whether from personal choice or because everyone shunned him, I never knew.

Sometime in the night there was a very loud crash and both Nolan and I came out of our blankets and out of the truck and into a gun-tub just behind our truck. Nolan, who had inflated his life belt, yelled that we had been torpedoed and started to go over the side of the ship but I grabbed him and told him we should wait to be sure as the water was so cold we probably wouldn't survive long enough to get to the beach. Slowly, some sailors appeared on deck with hooded flashlights and we discovered that due to the violent motion of the ship, one of the two and a half ton trucks on the deck had broken the tie-down chains on one side and had tipped over. We all pitched in to tie it down on it's side and Nolan and I got back into our truck and I, at least, slept soundly for the rest of the night. Nolan didn't, he kept his life-belt inflated and worried all night. He woke me from a sound sleep at dawn and said I'd better come take a look. I unwrapped myself from my cocoon of blankets and dismounted from the truck to face an awesome sight. There was no sky—just racing, ragged gray clouds. I looked all around the horizon and could see only gray-green moving mountains of water.

18

The ship was riding at anchor with taut chains off the bow and the seas coming from that direction looked like walls of water. The bow would rise like an elevator to meet them, but occasionally wouldn't quite make it to the top before it would plunge into the wall and water would come rushing down the deck, knee deep, to crash into the superstructure just as the stern would sluggishly start to rise. Looking aft toward the beach, we could see, from the crest of the waves, monstrous destruction. There was no artificial dock any more; there were ships of some kind right up on the beach, sideways, but most terrifying of all was what looked like the bottom of an LST rising and falling not 500 yards away from us. The water was filled with flotsam and jetsam, including bodies floating face down, kept from sinking by inflated lifebelts. One of the Coast Guard Officers came out on deck, probably surprised to see a soldier who wasn't seasick. He told me that the seas were running more than 50 feet high and we would just have to wait the storm out before they could put us on the beach. He told me that what looked like a capsized ship was indeed and that when their mooring chains had broken sometime in the night, the ship had gotten crossways of the seas and with the heavy deck load it had capsized. He didn't know if there were any survivors or not. He said as far as he knew, all of the people in our company were sick and that most of the ship's crew were sick also except for himself and three or four other men. This officer was an Ensign, about my age and, I guess, just about as scared as I was, otherwise he wouldn't have been talking to an enlisted man

I stood as far forward as I could, up in an elevated gun-tub in the bow, for a long time. The wind howled around me with so much noise that I could hear nothing else. I had to hang on tight for the water would occasionally come over the bow with tremendous force and I would take the heavy spray, but I couldn't be wetter than I already was so I just rode up and down like I was on a very fast elevator. The bow would drop out from under me and then go up again with so much speed that my knees would jack. I finally gave up and went back to the compartment we had been assigned as a rest area. Sergeant Gruber, the Mess Sergeant was there and asked me if I would help him down below on the tank deck as everyone else was sick. We went below where there was an immense pile of rations at the rear of the deck. We picked out case after case of canned chicken and stowed them into every niche and cranny we could find on our trucks. Sergeant Gruber said he didn't know whether the rations belonged to the Army or Coast Guard, but he figured that as soon as the ship got back to England they could get more, but we were going to go further and further from the source and you never knew when extra rations would come in handy. He was right. Without those rations we would have lived on C-rations for the first three or four weeks in Normandy. C-rations were drab, dreary meals-in-a-package that were issued to us when our kitchen was unable to operate and when we were out surveying. Each ration contained a can of something—Stew, Hash, Beans or Egg and Potato, then there was a can of crackers, powdered coffee, three cigarettes and a candy bar. We all got sick of one thing or another and swapped with someone who was sick of something that we could tolerate. I hated the stew, it reminded me of dog-food, and swapped it for beans, I could eat the beans three times a day and frequently did. It was eerie, working down there on the tank deck and not a little scary. When the ship plunged into the seas there would be an enormously loud crash as the water battered the doors at the bow and I fervently hoped that they would hold for I thought I would much rather be on the top deck if the ship got into trouble. We finished the job, though, and I retired to my truck and tried to convince Nolan that he wasn't going to die from seasickness. I spent another comfortable night "rocked in the cradle of the deep" and Nolan spent the night bent over the rail, looking the fishes in the eye, and calling on his God to take him to heaven, or hell, and end his suffering. That Nolan! Always complaining, There we were on a nice comfortable ship, with a nice dry, soft place to sleep and plenty of fresh air and nobody shooting at us and he was complaining.

By the next morning the seas had subsided to the point where we were going to land. We all took our assigned stations as the sailors took in the anchors and the ship headed toward the beach.

20

The ship came closer and closer, dropping stern anchors to aid in backing off after they had unloaded us. We could feel the drag as it grounded in the sand and then we had to wait several hours for the tide to uncover the beach off the bow. There was wreckage strewn everywhere, much of it from the storm that we had just survived, but a great deal still left from D-Day, two weeks before. No one had time to pick up wreckage, it was just bulldozed aside and passed by. There was a dead sailor floating at the side of our ship. Nolan said he had seen dead sailors at the other two invasions of Africa and Sicily as well. As the huge bow doors were opening a German plane came screaming down the beach, it was an FW-190 firing its wing-mounted cannon. A sailor jumped into the forward gun-tub and started pulling off the canvas cover of the twin 20 mm guns there. He yelled at me to get in there and help him but I decided, in a big hurry, "Hey, that ain't my job, man," and ran to get under something, like a big, heavy truck engine. The German flyer must have been either inexperienced or scared because otherwise it would seem to have been next to impossible to miss all those LST's standing there on the beach, but miss he did. He hadn't gotten far when a swarm of American P-51's were all over him like fleas on a dog and down he went in a big cloud of black smoke, far up the beach toward the British positions.

I rode our three-quarter ton truck through the water at the end of the ramp and onto the beach. There were occasional shells coming from the Germans, not aimed at anyone or anything, as they had no way of observing the fall of their shells, so it was just a display of Teutonic bad temper. Our company formed up in column on the beach and we rode up through one of the hard fought-over beach exits at Vierville sur Mere. As we crested the hill and headed for our assigned camp area inland, I looked back at the beach with all the ships, trucks, tanks, artillery and men—living and dead, and the picture was etched into my memory forever.

Riding through the trough onto Omaha Beach. Roger on the left, Wilton Hall, Charlie Smith, Lawson Dean (back of Smith) Can't rember the driver's name. I was astonished when I found this picture in a publication. Note the big smiles on our faces - probably because we weren't being shot at.

Normandy

As our truck convoy crested the hill and left Omaha Beach behind, I tried to look forward to see what was ahead but, fortunately, I could not. We passed through a couple of small hamlets and at a larger town, Isigny, we turned onto the road to St. Lo. Our camp was in an orchard in the Bocage country several miles up that road, near a little village called La Foret. We were

22

*This photo of Omaha Beach must have been taken about June 22,
just after the big storm. In the foreground can be seen stacks of
bridging material; on the left, mid-picture, there appears to be an
LCI (Landing Craft Infantry) high and dry. Note the trough of
water which all vehicles had to go through.*

isolated from the rest of the world by a hedgerow that surrounded the orchard.

Our only neighbors were members of a 90 mm antiaircraft battery and their vicious guns. We were supposed to feel safer, having these guns to protect us from air attack, but the problem was that what goes up---must come down. When those 90s fired, we all ran to get under a truck engine, because the fragments from those bursting shells attained terminal velocity on their way back down and would penetrate anything but a nice big chunk of metal. The secondary problem was that there were not enough truck engines to accommodate all of us. I became known as the fastest runner in the company. They said that I once went sliding, feet first, like a base stealer, under an engine so fast that my steel helmet came off in mid-air and before it hit the ground I reached out and grabbed it Well, I <u>was</u> fast in those days, and that is a fact.

Nolan and I pitched our tent under an apple tree that had shortly before been in full bloom. It took the rest of the day to set up the camp—headquarters tent, mess tent, platoon tents, press trucks, photo mapping trucks, dig and set up latrine shelter tents, etc. By the time we finished it was beginning to get dark and I had guard duty. That very first night we set a pattern that was to last for months to come. There was one guard post at the entrance/exit of the orchard and a roving post around the camp and back to the entrance. As the people settled down and the camp became quiet we could hear the occasional bang of a mortar round or artillery shell up ahead of us. It sounded as if the explosions were about a couple of miles away, but sounds were always muffled and distorted by the myriad hedgerows that enclosed small fields, orchards or pastures. About midnight I was scared by the very distinctive whooshing of a shell passing over. It was the first one I had heard, so I flattened myself on the ground and waited for the explosion. Nothing. I got up sheepishly, glad it was dark and nobody had seen my cowardly performance. Shortly thereafter I heard that whooshing sound again, but this time I just crouched slightly instead of prostrating myself. Again I heard no explosion subsequent to the whooshing. I resumed my walking on the soft grass and listened intently to see if I could hear a gun going off, but the whooshing came and went again with neither sound of gun nor explosion of impact. Finally I came to the conclusion that the shell I heard going over was fired by a large naval gun off-shore and was probably landing 10 or 15 miles inland, thus all I heard was its whispering, subsonic passage, a mile or so overhead.

The next day I was detailed out with a survey party to start surveying on the St. Lo highway. I was the only PFC in the party so my job was sort of like a spear carrier in an opera. Had we been a Hollywood movie crew I would have been the "gopher". The Sergeants had the staring roles, Lieutenant Wilkinson ("Wilkie") was the director and I was the gopher. "Hey Aldrich, go for this. Hey Aldrich, go for that." I didn't mind, for I could see that I really was the most important person in the party, for without me to "gopher" stuff the whole war effort would have ground to a halt. Besides, it gave me time to see the country and explore, as long as I stayed within sight and sound of the sergeant in charge. There were a lot of rules that the veterans drummed into my head. "Be careful where you step—look first, step second. Watch out for mines and trip wires. Touch nothing. Pick up nothing. It may be booby-trapped. If it's valuable like a pistol or dirk, tie a string to it, back off and yank the string sharply. If nothing blows up it probably is safe. If you find something valuable we all share it. If it's worthless, it's yours."

The first day, we went up the road to our starting point in our ¾ ton weapons carrier and a jeep. Both vehicles mounted 30 cal. machine guns and we each carried a slung carbine. The vehicles stayed behind as we surveyed along the road. When we disappeared from the drivers' sight they moved up to where they could see us and waited until we disappeared again. We were not combat troops, but we were expected to use our weapons to defend ourselves. We were always moving toward the front and the closer we came to it the more dangerous our situation became. The "front" was not usually a well-established, static line like the World War I trenches, but was rather a fluid, sometimes invisible place. If we heard small arms firing ahead, we stopped to investigate. The scary part was not hearing anything, for then the enemy could be anywhere—in our front, to our side or behind us.

As we worked our way up the road I spotted a dead German soldier in the ditch and went closer to take a look. This was the first German corpse that I had seen and I wanted to see his face, wondering mildly if he could be one of my German acquaintances from my Youth Hostel days. There was no face to look at. To my horror, he had no head at all, just the bloody, torn stump of a neck. This was my introduction to violent death. At that time, death of any kind was a stranger to me. My Grandfather Aldrich had died when I was twelve and my cousin Myrtle Straw, had died a couple of years later and I had attended their funerals. As much as I can recall these were the only deaths or dead people that I had seen up to the time of our landing on Omaha Beach. From that point on, death was to be my constant companion. Dead German soldiers. Dead American Soldiers. Dead French civilians. Dead cows, dead horses, dead pigs, dead poultry, dead dogs, dead cats. Everywhere—everyday—death. The stench of death filled my nostrils every waking minute. When I awoke from sleep, I could smell it. There was no escape from it. The further up the St. Lo road we went, the more dead we came across. There were bodies everywhere—in the ditches, in the fields and pastures on the hedgerows. One body haunted me for years. He had been killed by a mine and his body was blown from the sunken lane up into the shrubbery at the top of the hedgerow. He was in an upright position, head forward on his chest, arms thrown out and held spread-eagled by thorns in the shrubbery. If one ignored the dirty, blood-stained uniform he resembled Christ on the Cross. We worked, almost constantly, out ahead of the Graves Registration units whom we would sometimes see picking up bodies as we came back to the camp for the night. Frequently we would pass the same bodies day after day, their sightless eyes staring at us, accusing us, pleading with us. I knew I could do nothing for them and that left an even bigger hurt in me. I would stare into the dark in my tent and would see those eyes again and again. They were all so young.

Every day during June and July, we surveyed closer and closer to St. Lo. And every day there were more and more bodies to pass. Usually when we first passed them they would look as if they were sleeping, albeit in strange positions. By the second or third day they would be swollen and grotesque, their flesh straining their uniforms almost to the point of bursting. Occasionally, incoming German artillery shells would further insult these dead by shredding them into some unrecognizable shape wrapped in brown or gray rags. The road was under sporadic artillery fire, for while not much of it was under direct observation, the dust rising from a passing vehicle would anger the Germans and they would fire at what they thought was the base of the dust plume. The vehicle drivers would push their vehicles to the limit and tear down this stretch of road one at a time, spaced one or two minutes apart. The white dust would rise into the air and we would hear the whine of those shells coming in. Almost invariably there would be nothing at the base of the plume but us. We would dive into the ditch, do our best to crawl completely inside our steel helmets and wait for the second or third salvo to walk closer and closer, up the road toward us.

I'm sure that most people have seen exploding shells in a movie or on television. Don't believe it. When a shell explodes in daylight the only thing visible is a puff of black smoke. When you see all that fire in the movies remember that it is produced by gasoline or flash powder, because the directors don't think you will believe an explosion that produces nothing but black smoke. If you wanted to incinerate someone during WWII, the shell of choice was white phosphorous, which, when it exploded, produced a beautiful fountain effect. The burning fragments consumed anything they touched and could not be extinguished except by smothering with dirt or sand. So, don't believe those big movie explosions, they never happened.

I saw the first and only General that I ever saw, on that road one day. We were just picking ourselves up out of the ditch after the "Nasties" had fired another salvo of "88's" on us, when a jeep bearing a two-star flag stopped beside us. The General, I never did find out who he was, asked us if the road went to St. Lo. Our Tech-Sgt. answered, "Yes, Sir." and we all dove for the ditch again as we could hear the 88's coming in. The General's driver turned the jeep around abruptly, and headed, at high speed, back in the other direction. Our Tennessee comedian said in his slow drawl, "Who was that Masked Man, anyhow?" and we all chorused, "Hi Yo Silver, Away" and rolled on the ground laughing.

I, for one, did not expect to survive this daily lethal hailstorm. Each morning after breakfast, I would say to myself, "Well, today may be the day. Your last living day on earth. Oh, God. Are you there? Or have you left us?" I would gather the threads of my courage together and get into the truck. None of us talked or joked on our way up the road. We sat there, staring introspectively at nothing, each with his own thoughts.

Triangulation station on a Normandy hilltop. Roger on right.

I shouldn't say that this happened everyday for there were occasions when our officers felt that because the front was static we would not be able to carry our traverse survey any further forward. On a few of those infrequent days we might be given the afternoon off to go to Isigny or Carentan. I was in one of those towns one afternoon, I think it was Isigny, strolling around looking at closed shops and damaged buildings. I stopped at a World War I memorial monument and was painstakingly translating the inscriptions when an elderly man asked me a question. My French was pretty good in those days and after I asked him to repeat the question, "S'il vous plait" I found that if I paid close attention to him I could understand him well enough. He pointed to a name on the monument and told me that it was his son, nineteen years old, killed in 1916. He said that he was very glad to see the Americans here again and he wished me all the best in the world. There were rose bushes in full bloom at the base of the monument. The elderly gentleman reached over, plucked one red rose and gave it to me saying, "Au 'voir, Monsieur Soldat, vas tu avec le Bon Dieu." I stood there with the rose in my hand, staring at the young, bronze Poilu with fixed bayonet, forever fending off the invader. With tears running down my cheeks, I watched the very gracious, stoop shouldered old man walk away.

There were times when the front was static, and we couldn't carry our traverse any further without endangering the crew, we worked at triangulation. Triangulation, for the uninitiated is a method of ascertaining precise distances. From a very carefully measured base line we turned angles and by knowing the measurement of one side of a triangle and the angles formed by sighting on some distant object the measurement of the other two sides can be determined. We worked from the summits of hills, church spires, water towers, etc. This was a slow, laborious process which entailed the turning of the same angles over and over again and then taking an average of the accumulated readings. Once again, I had plenty of time to talk with farmers, their wives and children, and plenty of time to observe. I used to swap cigarettes and candy bars with the Norman farmers or their wives, for fresh eggs and little new potatoes. We would fry them for our lunch over a small gasoline fire in a ration can. We always carried a frying pan, liberated from some wrecked house, in the truck. I once complimented a farm woman on the beauty of her little children.

29

She told me that they were not hers, but Jewish children that she had volunteered to take in as her own from a Jewish family in the village who expected to be taken prisoner by the Germans. She said that indeed, the Jewish family had been taken, but she was raising the children as her own, not knowing whether their parents would ever be back to claim them. I wondered if the beauty, generosity and love of some people could ever make up for the cruelty and bestiality of others? Does it balance? I had seen hundreds, if not thousands, of dead American soldiers there. They didn't know these French people. They had no real, compelling reason to be here other than an idealistic one. Yet they had given up their lives so that the French could be free of an oppressor. Who would take care of their children? There was no answer.

American soldiers, like all soldiers anywhere, I suppose, were always looking for alcoholic beverages. The kind or brand didn't matter—just the alcohol content. The idea was to buy a few hours or minutes of euphoric feeling and to escape the horrors of war. The men of our company, being veterans of two other campaigns, were like pigs hunting truffles, they could smell alcohol from a mile away. They could sniff it out if it was buried. Bloodhounds had nothing on these guys when it came to finding alcohol. Since I could speak French I was the one to ask the farm people, "Avez vous du cidre?" We filled jerry cans (a jerry can was a 5 gal. can used for water, gasoline or other liquid) with the stuff, took it back to the company and swapped for more cigarettes and candy to be used to acquire more cider. War or no war, living in Normandy had its advantages. Then one memorable day a farmer said yes he had cider, but he also had Calvados. None of us knew what Calvados was so we said, "OK, let's try it." It looked like white wine but looks was as far as any resemblance went. Calvados, is a high-powered apple brandy, distilled from "hard" cider. I once made the mistake of filling my canteen with the stuff. A year later I could still taste it through the heavily chlorinated water. This black-market enterprise soon came to a screeching halt when Capt. Kent found out where all the booze was coming from. Of course he also found out the reason why there was so much festivity going on after working hours. Further on in this story I'll tell you about the time, after the war was over in Europe, when we found a German Army warehouse, loaded to the roof with 5 gal. demijohns of French brandy. It still boggles my mind.

The knowledgeable veterans in our outfit frowned on souvenir hunting, but on occasion we all indulged in it. While in Normandy, we once found a couple of crates of German "Potato Masher" grenades; the grenades in one crate were live and the other crate held practice grenades. The practice grenades had holes drilled through the head so that if you held them up to the light you could see through them, otherwise they were identical to the real and deadly grenades. Usually, in order to take advantage of all the daylight, we worked so long that the other men in the company would have already started supper when we got back. No matter how tired, dirty and haunted we were, we would have to get on the tail end of the line and wait for all the rest to get through before we could take our turn. The big disadvantage of all this was that if the cooks had managed to whip up something that we were particularly fond of, by the time we finished our firsts, the seconds would be all gone. On our way back to camp on the day that we found the grenades our T-Sgt. said, "Well boys, we're going to be at the head of the line tonight." When we pulled into camp the sergeant pulled one of the practice grenades from its crate and tucked it into his belt. We headed toward the front of the chow line and as we got near the sergeant pulled the grenade out, waved it around over his head, and shouted, "Look what we found!", with that he very ostentatiously pulled the cord from the grenade handle and tossed it into the chow line. There was a mad scramble to get away from there, people tripped and went flat, people dropped their mess gear in the dirt, people ran into each other and lost their helmets and there was much terrified yelling and hollering. When the dust settled and the allotted time for an explosion had passed without any occurring, there were the six of us standing at the head of the line with our mess kits open. There were some challenges to fight and many imprecations, but our sergeant said, "Be calm, boys. We've got lots more grenades and some of them are real. So the next time we come back to the area tired and hungry, be nice people and let us into the front of the line. If you don't, you ain't going to know which one is going to explode and which one isn't." The sergeant had the ability to intimidate almost anyone and this time his effort paid off for his crew. With much grumbling and catcalling the line always parted for us thereafter, with our Tech-Sgt. leading us up front with a swagger, sort of like Moses leading his people through the Red Sea.

One evening after chow, some of us were reading in the rec. tent, the only spot with electric lights available to us lower ranks, when we heard a commotion outside and turned out to investigate. It seemed that Lt. "Wilkie" had been entertaining the rest of the lieutenants with some of the liquid refreshments that his surveyors had brought back and they had decided to try out some of the German "potato-masher" grenades that we had also brought back. The argument was about where to explode them. We all listened with a respectful(?) silence, back out of sight in the dark shadows, while they argued about the place. Much to our astonishment, they chose the officers' latrine, a one-holer. We all groaned, knowing who would have to clean up the mess, and moved back another 50 feet or so. One of them, I think it was Lt. Tokarz, pulled the cord and dropped the grenade in the hole and they all ran out of range. There is a hoary old joke, very crude and coarse, but riotously funny to a group of soldiers, the punch line goes, "Where were you when the s--- hit the fan?" We changed it to, "Where were you when the grenade hit the can?"

I have a couple of old, dog-eared photos of some of us surveyors up on a hill in Normandy. We were doing triangulation up there on a pleasant, warm summer's day. No artillery shells, no dead soldiers, no smell of death except for a few dead cows. On our maps there were two trail-like roads that led to the summit of the hill. For some unknown reason the sergeants and Lt. Wilkie had chosen the northern road. There was evidence that the Germans had used the road and hill, no doubt as an observation point. We worked from the summit all day. When it came time to go back to our camp, the Lieutenant and Tech Sgt. Dwyer had a mild argument

32

about whether we would return by the same road that we used to come up, or go down by the other road which looked as if the

Our survey crew on that Norman hilltop. L. To R., front row, Charlie Smith, Wilton Hall, Second row - Sgt. Little, Lawson Dean, Sgt. Dwyer, Lt. Wilkinson (Wilkie), 3rd row - Roger, Stan Olshefski, Cpl. McCartney.

Germans had used it more frequently. They finally agreed to go down the way we came. When we got to the point where the other road exited onto the main road we saw a company of combat engineers removing mines from it. Had we gone down that other road none of us would have gotten back for supper. This was the first in a remarkable chain of escapes that was to follow us for the next year. As I said earlier, I don't believe in spirits, or the hand of fate. I thought then, and I think now, that it is too much to ask of God to follow any one person or small group of persons around and keep them from harm while at the same time ignoring the thousands who are going to be killed. So I am left with no other answer as to why we lived and others died, except random chance. But if it was random chance, the odds on our winning the lottery with death must have been mighty small by the end of the war.

On the fourth of July every gun on our front fired at 12 noon. One monstrous salute. It made a lot more noise than we kids used to at home. It must have bewildered the Germans. A few nights later, just after dark, we heard an increasing volume of small arms fire in front of us. We were behind the 29th and 30th Divisions and it became apparent that they were receiving an attack and by the sound it seemed to be headed our way. Capt. Kent ordered everyone out onto the hedgerows surrounding our camp, we set up all our machine guns, anti-tank bazookas and carbines and waited. Eventually we could hear voices shouting and the distinctive sound of Schmieser machine pistols but the sounds died down and word came back that the attack had been contained less than one half mile from us. This was on July 10th and we found out later that 2 battalions of the 902nd Panzer Grenadier regiment had smashed into the 119th and 120th Infantry regiments of the 30th Division and had gotten well into the 119th's rear area before being stopped.

Sgt. Little at a Normandy triangulation station

Saint Lo

The attack on St. Lo began the next day. By July 18 the city had been taken, but enemy artillery fire was so intense that scarcely anything could move. By the 20th or so we were extending our traverse into the city although there was still some house-to-house fighting. St. Lo was a small city. It had been almost totally destroyed by artillery fire first from the Americans and then the Germans. I don't know if it had also been bombed but the damage could not have been more complete even if it had been. My impression of it is that there were scarcely two stones left together and photos that were taken at about the same time that we were there bear this out. There were bodies of both Americans and Germans strewn through the rubble. There were bodies of French civilians there also and the ever-present smell of death was stronger there than in any other place in Normandy. We worked our way deeper into the city on a street that entered the city square, a large open space, in front of a ruined church.

Ruined church in St. Lo

There were infantrymen standing around in the street, but we paid no attention. I think I was one of the rodmen that day, that is, I held a wooden rod with foot and inch marks painted on it. The instrument man sighted on it to turn his angle from the backsight. The chainmen measured the distance with a 100 ft. steel tape and one of the guys had a notebook in which he recorded angles and distances. So there were six of us in the survey party, leap frogging along—front rod became back rod and then moved forward to be front rod again. We moved at our usual slow pace out of the protection of the street into the open space of the square but we hadn't gotten very far when a Schmieser machine pistol opened up on us from some building on the other side of the square. Bullets kicked up dirt around our feet and each of us dropped what we were holding and we all took off at a mad pace in six different directions. I came skidding around the corner of a building back into the street from which we had come. There was an infantry sergeant standing there who looked for all the world like Bill Mauldin's "Willey" character, and he said, in a laconic Texas drawl, "What's the matter, son? Kinda hot out there?" I was too embarrassed to answer and then he said, "We been hunting this guy all morning and we figured that you Engineers would probably be too much of a target for him to ignore. Did he get any of you?" I was astonished and angered that they had used us as bait. They hadn't even warned us. Only our incredible good luck had saved us. I knew better than to show any anger though. I mumbled something and peeked over his shoulder as he peered out into the square. We were just in time to see an explosion in one of the second floor windows across the square from us. He said they had some guys waiting with rifle grenades and as soon as the sniper had revealed his position by firing at us they had him spotted and fired the grenades. The only reason none of us was hit was that the Schmieser, which we called a "Burp" gun, fired so fast that it was next to impossible to hit a swiftly moving target at the distance we were from him. And we were indeed, swiftly moving targets. Miraculous escape number two.

A few days after the St. Lo incident, we were standing in line for breakfast when we heard what sounded like hundreds of planes approaching. As we looked toward the west, we found that the noise was exactly that—hundreds and hundreds of bombers, B-25s, B-26s, B-17s, and B-24s—all in formation and heading right over us. The column of planes stretched away toward England like a vast, moving belt with no end in sight. They started dumping bombs when they were no more than three or four miles to our front. We could clearly see the bombs falling. We could also clearly see an agonizing amount of flack bursting around the planes. Several of the big bombers were hit. One plane lost a wing which fluttered down much like a maple tree seed-pod, keys we used to call them, the burning plane plunging down at a faster rate, its' explosion indistinguishable from all the other explosions. Some of the bombers went into slow flat spins. We were all yelling, "Get out! Jump! Come on, get out!" But not many of the fliers in those stricken bombers did. Gradually the intensity of the flack slackened, became sporadic and then quit altogether. The ground shook continuously where we were. Our trousers legs fluttered eerily. The planes kept coming, hour after hour, in that endless stream, dropped their bombs and then turned back for England. After awhile we became aware that the rising smoke and dust seemed to be getting somewhat nearer to us, but then the impact point seemed to move away from us again. We found out later that because the wind carried the smoke and dust, which was the bombardiers aiming point, toward us, the bombers kept bombing short and many Americans were killed by their own bombs. Fortunately they were alerted to the mistake before they got anywhere near us. The bombing stopped sometime in late afternoon and then the guns opened up again. The next day we heard that our troops had broken through the hole in the German lines and were on the way south, out of Normandy. A few days later we were ordered to pack up, leave our peaceful orchard and follow behind the fast-moving infantry and armor.

A convoy moving through St. Lo After the battle

The road our convoy moved on went through St. Lo. Because of the rubble and the congestion of vehicles our pace was slow. Sitting alone, on the barracks bags, in the back of our weapons carrier, I had time to contemplate the still smoking ruins of St. Lo once more. I felt as though I was exiting a vast stage-set. This was the last scene, depicting Armageddon, and all of the actors had moved off stage, and all of the audience had left, except me. As we moved away I watched a ubiquitous two-and-a-half ton army truck move in the opposite direction, back toward the beaches. It was loaded to the top of the stakes with bloated American bodies, piled four or five deep, one on top of the other, like cord-wood. Each time the wheels hit a pot-hole the pile of bodies jounced up and down like some obscene pudding. St. Lo will never leave my memory. It sits there like a collection of ancient sepia colored photographic prints. I take them out and look at them once in a while.

Mount St. Michel

Once we got out of St. Lo and on a road to the south we made good progress. By nightfall we were a few miles South of Avranches, sleeping on the ground in our bed-rolls, sans tents. The next morning Capt. Kent said that some of us could take half a day off to visit Mount St. Michel if we wished and catch up with the

convoy later in the day. There were only six or eight of us who were interested. The rest of the company were not intellectually inclined that day, or most days, for that matter. When we arrived at "Le Mount", we found only one other small group of Americans there

Mt. St. Michel and Normandy impressions by Henry J. Mac-Millan, Combat Artist, assigned to the 62nd Eng. Co. Reproduced by photo/offset process by the 62nd Eng. Co.

41

ahead of us. The villagers told us we were the first Americans there, so essentially we had liberated the place. They brought out wine and toasted us liberally, but a couple of us were more interested in touring the monastery. A man who had been a guide there before the war escorted our two small groups around, talking to me and I interpreted for the rest. I was most impressed with the huge drum-shaped wheel upon which a monstrous rope was wound. The rope hauled a huge wicker basket up through a rock-cut shaft. The basket was used to carry up building materials, food and important people back in the medieval times. The power to wind the rope on the drum was furnished by prisoners or slaves walking inside the drum. Our guide offered to demonstrate if we would climb into the wheel but we declined the honor. I had visited several cathedrals in Britain so I could appreciate the architecture of the cathedral and monastery there at the Mount. It was a very enjoyable break from the war.

We caught up with the convoy at the evening camp site and were told to set up for an indefinite stay. That night we heard a lot of gunfire a little way to our north and found the next day that a serious German counter attack had been stopped just a few miles from Avranches. Had it succeeded all of the troops south of Avranches would have been cut off from the main body of the army. Our survey platoon started working that same day. We were in a part of the country that was similar to the downs along the south coast of England, steeply rolling country with the roads in the valleys. As we worked our way up this particular valley, a lone P-47 patrolling over us dove on something in the next valley to our left. He would disappear in back of the ridge, we would hear his guns firing, and he would climb steeply out, bank sharply and dive back into the valley again. We wondered why he was doing so much practice when he could be doing the real thing up ahead where the Germans were. Finally Lt. Wilkie told a couple of us to climb up the ridge and see what he was diving on. There was no path up the steep ridge side and we kept slipping on the short grass but with much huffing and puffing we arrived at the summit , winded and with pounding hearts. When we looked down we saw what the P-

47 pilot was diving on and our hearts pounded even harder. He had just released a bomb on a German tank and it was burning furiously. There was another tank, right behind the first, trying to turn around on the narrow road. Both tanks were "buttoned up" to deflect the machine gun fire so no one in the second tank saw us. As he tried to turn around he was maybe two or three hundred feet below us, and so close that we could have hit him with a rock. We dropped on our bellies and, foolishly, started firing our carbines at the tank which was so close we couldn't possibly miss. Our shots went pinging away after ricocheting off the tank. Obviously our little 30 cal. pea shooters weren't going to do anything but annoy the tankers, but they couldn't elevate any of their guns high enough to shoot back and at least, they wouldn't dare to open the hatch and jump out. We hadn't gotten off more than three or four shots each when the P-47 came hurtling back, dropped his second bomb and the tank went up in a cloud of flame and smoke. I doubt if the pilot of the P-47 ever saw the two of us dancing and capering around with glee, up there on the ridge. Lt. "Wilkie" figured from our actions that whatever had happened, the outcome must be O.K., so he yelled at us to come down and report. He was mad with us for firing on the tank, but after awhile he could see the humor of it and broke out laughing at the thought of his two privates attacking a German Mark-4 tank all by themselves with a couple of carbines. He had a couple of heroes on his hands. We never got any medals for it though. As a matter of fact, the Captain was heard to remark that since we were only a private and a PFC he couldn't very well bust us down in rank for having so much fun, even if we had done such a dumb thing. First and only time I ever hit anything with that carbine too.

Paris

We marked time there while the American and British Armies tried to trap the Germans at Falaise. Once that battle was over, the few Germans that were left alive went streaming back toward their homeland and we started to move again as well. We passed by Paris a few miles to our East and as we passed Capt. Kent allowed half the company to go in for half a day and the other half to go in

On the day we went to Paris. Note the complete absence of vehicles. One of my buddies, "Happy" Forte in foreground.

the next day. Paris had been liberated only a few days before, they hadn't even had the victory parade yet. We parked our trucks on the back side of the hill, below the Arc de Triomphe and walked through the Arch to go down the Champs Elysees. I'm sure you have all heard the expression that "Everyone should be able to be famous for fifteen minutes." Well, let me tell you it was more fun to be a hero for half a day. It seemed as if half of the women in Paris hugged and kissed us that day. We were quite literally dragged into bars and told that not to drink a toast with the French people was an insult. We decided that it would be unpatriotic to insult our allies so close to their day of liberation. I managed to stay sober enough to get to the Eiffel Tower, but couldn't go up for the elevators weren't operating. I remember a bunch of us sitting on the curb to rest and watch the beautiful young women ride by on their bicycles. In those days, when French women rode bicycles they didn't sit on their skirts, but tossed them over the saddle so that they wouldn't wear the skirt out, materials being so scarce and expensive. Riding a bike like that allowed an amazing amount of thigh to show. We sat there on the curb and cheered as they rode by—the higher the skirt, the louder we cheered. They smiled and waved at us and seemed not the least bit offended. It had been a long war for everyone and it was nice to have something to cheer about. We wearily ran the gauntlet of bars and women, back up the Champs Elysees to our trucks and caught up with the company about supper time. The Capt. looked us over and decided that none of us was in any condition to do guard duty, so he told us to sleep it off.

I never went back to Paris. I could have gone back on a pass, but I cherished the memories of that day when I was a hero and everything was free. That opportunity came only once in a lifetime in France. After that one time you were a "charge-em-double" tourist, even if you were in uniform.

Belgium

We crossed northern France rapidly. I remember going through St. Quentin, for the name stuck in my mind as the namesake place of St. Quentin prison in California. When I was in California in 1938 with the American Youth Hostel, we once talked with some St. Quentin prisoners on a road construction gang in Sequoia Park. I remember seeing signs directing one to the old WW I battlegrounds, Chateau Theirry, Belliue Wood, etc. I wanted to stop and be a tourist but we rolled right on through. When we crossed the Belgian boarder, The Belgians made sure that we knew we were in Belgium rather than France. They waved Belgian flags and shouted, "Nous somme Belgique."

The German resistance stiffened about the time we got to Belgium and we slowed our mad dash from place to place. Still, us privates seldom knew where we really were. Once, after traveling in convoy all day, we pulled off the road after dark. First Sgt. Leach placed Nolan and me on guard and personally conducted us to our post for the night. We had a 50 cal. machine gun, mounted on a jeep as our weapon. Our orders were that one of us could sleep in a bed roll beside the jeep while the other watched for the enemy, and we were to stay there until we were relieved. The rest of the company were camped at some unknown place ahead of us, or behind us, depending on which way we were looking. I've never known such a dark night, before or since. Sitting at the trigger end of the machine gun, I could not see the end of the barrel. So there we were. Nothing to eat except C rations. No way to heat them. As a matter of fact, we had no way of knowing what we were eating other than the taste. I think I had a can of hash for supper, with tepid canteen water to wash it down. I took the first watch and Nolan curled up on the ground and slept, snoring loudly. Had the enemy been within five miles of us they surely would have heard him.

We had one watch with a luminescent dial so when my two hours were up, I woke Nolan, gave him the watch and fell into a deep sleep immediately. I had not slept more than a minute or two when Nolan woke me, "Roger, wake up. I hear something." I sat up and listened but heard nothing unusual so I went back to sleep— for a minute or two. "Wake up, Roger. There's that noise again. I'm going to shoot." I said, "No, no. Don't shoot. Wait and see if we can figure out what it is."

I didn't get any more sleep during Nolan's two-hour shift. I had to keep him from firing that monstrous machine gun. My turn came again but I couldn't hear a thing over the infernal racket of Nolan's snoring. After an interminable two hours Nolan took over again, and again he woke me, threatening to shoot at whatever it was that he heard. He insisted there were hundreds of Germans creeping up on us. I finally got exasperated and said, "For God's sake, Nolan, will you keep your mouth shut and let me sleep?" I might as well have been talking to a frightened little child, which, I guess, was essentially what he was. I didn't get to sleep more than five uninterrupted minutes all night. Dawn came on slowly despite the thick, lowery clouds, and Nolan became more insistent. Now he not only could hear the enemy, but he could see them moving. I wearily got out of my blankets, stood up and looked—"They're cows you God Damned idiot. Cows. You've kept me awake all night over a bunch of stupid cows." I opened a can of beans and had my breakfast, wondering if I could kill Nolan and bury him there and be done with him forever. Sgt. Leach came down the grassy lane and interrupted my thoughts. We were relieved and went back to the convoy..

Our group of surveyors moved up to help some artillerymen check the coordinates for a 240 mm howitzer they were setting up. We went into a nearby church and climbed the ladders up into the belfry. The Sergeant had us rig a platform up above the bells, at a point where we could knock tiles off the steeple and see out in a circle with the theodolite. The weather was turning colder and in order to warm up someone built a small fire on the slate floor of the belfry. We heated water to have some instant coffee. When we left, late in the afternoon, we poured our canteens onto the fire and extinguished it. When we came back the next morning to resume our work, the church had burned. We asked some of the artillery guys what had happened and one of them said, "Dunno. We woke up in the night and the whole place was on fire. Must have been hit by a shell, but we didn't hear nothin'." We got back in our jeeps and drove off. Sgt. Little said, "Remind me not to have coffee in a belfry again."

When we arrived in France in June we had to make drastic changes in our life style. In England we could take a shower whenever we wanted in the bath hut where we also shaved and washed. In France a shower once a week was a luxury. On a designated day we piled into our trucks and drove to wherever our Corp Quartermasters had set up a shower tent. For shaving and washing each day we drew a quart of hot water from our kitchen, carried in our steel helmet. That was it. Wash your feet, your body, shave and shampoo - all with that one quart. I don't remember what happened about laundry, but I know we had to wash our own socks and I seem to remember that we got clean clothes (i.e. shirt and trousers) once a week.

Holland

We moved out of Belgium and into Holland. We were in a little place called "Gulpen" which is in the southern "panhandle" of Holland. We moved into yet another farmer's orchard. They must have hated to see us coming. While we were in Gulpen the autumn rains started and our big trucks, loaded with paper coming in and loaded with maps going out, soon turned the orchard into a quagmire. It became necessary to winch them in and winch them out again. Our pup-tents became dreary places to spend the night. I had, by this time become an experienced scrounger, and had acquired another shelter-half and had a tent to myself. I thought that maybe I was finally rid of Nolan, but he got himself another tent half and set his tent up within a foot of mine. I had requested my waxed canvas sleeping bag cover from home and it had arrived in good time. I now had four blankets instead of the issued two, and by folding them together and stuffing them into the sleeping bag cover I had a reasonably warm sleeping nest until the weather started deteriorating at a rapid pace. It became necessary to wrap my rain-coat around the foot of my bed-roll to keep the rain from soaking through. It became further necessary to add my overcoat on top of the bed-roll to preserve more body heat. Then instead of sleeping in my underwear as prescribed by the army, I started sleeping in my clothes, adding a sweater and a woolen cap, and two pairs of socks and a pair of woolen gloves. We discovered that shivering helps, by forcing the body to warm up. There came a morning when I felt warmer, but felt something heavy pressing down on me. Turning over I discovered that the tent was down on me, pushed there by snow! Pulling on my boots, I crawled out to find that we had 10 inches of heavy, wet snow. Conditions which had been merely intolerable before now became infinitely worse than that. Mud mixed with snow makes a most undesirable living environment.

While we were in this spot we were visited each night by a most persistent "Bed-check Charlie." We hadn't been visited by him since Normandy. Bed-check Charlie was what we called any German night-time observation plane. The people in the plane were looking for lights or if it was a moonlit night they could spot trucks moving. When Charlie came over the night after it snowed, he apparently spotted our truck tracks, for while he was overhead German artillery started coming in on us. We all started running for cover. Lt. Wilkie tripped on the curbing of the farmers manure pit and fell in headfirst. We urged him stay down-wind of us for a couple of weeks after that. Our permanent KP, Earl, fell over a barbed wire fence and got a nasty gash in his leg requiring stitches to close. The Officers put him in for a Purple Heart medal and he actually received the award—the only one in our company during the entire war.

The area around Gulpen was dotted with sandstone mines and quarries. In a weak moment, I had acquired a Schmieser machine pistol from a dead German soldier, and a group of us took it, one afternoon, to a nearby quarry to try it out. We had fired maybe two or three clips of ammo through it when we discovered heads appearing over the rim of the quarry walls, like Indians surrounding a wagon train. The distinctive sound of that "Burp" gun had scared a neighboring infantry company. Needless to say, we didn't try that gun out again and soon thereafter I traded it off for some other unremembered souvenir.

The attempt to capture Aachen, just over the border in Germany, was in full swing at this time. On a hill overlooking the city our surveying halted for we had run out of forward territory to survey. We were there on the day that the powers above decided that since the resistance to the attack was too heavy to overcome, they would bomb Aachen out of existence. The bomber stream came directly over our position on the hill. As the planes passed over us they would open their bomb-bay doors and the bombs would come tumbling out to travel in their arc into the smoke and dust caused by the previous bombs. Looking up into those open bomb-bay doors was an awesome sight and the city slowly disappeared in a huge cloud of rising smoke. We watched for a long time, having nothing better to do, but our passive show became too active. We were horrified to see a group of approaching bombers open their doors well before they got to our hill and the bombs

49

started falling much too soon. There was nowhere for us to hide so we watched the bombs descend with frightened fascination. They exploded, maybe a couple of hundred yards away from us and before the next flight got to us we mounted our jeeps and got out of there. We returned the next day to find that our hill-top position was covered with interlocking bomb craters. They missed us by only a few minutes.

Hotel Park Rooding, Valkenburg, Holland, Oct. 1944

Someone in the upper echelons decided that it was time for the 62nd to move into winter quarters a few days after the snow storm. We moved north a few miles to Valkenburg and into the Hotel Park Rooding. The Germans had used the same hotel for their headquarters a few weeks before. We were assigned rooms—two to a room. We were to eat in the hotel dining room—our cooks having taken over the kitchen. After we had settled into our rooms we were given the rest of the day off. Sleep was what we wanted. I put my bed roll on one of the beds and thought I would go immediately to sleep but no, I had slept too long on the hard ground. I pulled the mattress off onto the floor and slept for a straight 18 hours, ignoring both lunch and dinner. I could get food anytime, but I could never get enough sleep.

Valkenburg was a nice little town and the Dutch people were very friendly. There is a huge, ancient sandstone mine with several

An entrance to the sandstone mine in Valkenburg

entrances in Valkenburg. The mine has literally hundreds of miles of tunnels. One of our guys, Gulbenk, spoke fluent German, his parents brought him to the U.S. in 1936 or '37, and he could understand Dutch and make himself understood. We found a fellow who had guided tourists into the mines before the war, and for a small fee he took a few of us in, lighting our way by a large acetylene lantern, and explained what we were seeing. There were rooms hollowed out where people had taken refuge from Napoleon's troops and other wars since then. Parts of the mine went back to Charlemaigne's time, and it was all very fascinating. One day when we had some time off, Sgt Little, who used to be a mine surveyor in Pennsylvania, took Sgt. Dwyer and a couple of us Privates and we went into the mine with a jeep. I was scared to death that would never find our way out, but the Sgts. knew what they were doing, and we came out in another town about three miles away. We went to movies a couple of times in the local theater mixed in with the local Dutch people.

Valkenburg was on the flight path of one of Hitler's secret weapons, the V-1, Buzz Bomb. They were aimed at Antwerp, Belgium and as many as twenty or thirty of them would fly over us during the day. As you may know, the Buzz Bomb was a jet propelled bomb with stubby wings. It's engine, a ram jet, made a peculiar, unmistakable fluttering, putting, buzzing sound. They flew low over us, maybe as much as a thousand feet up, but not much more. When the guard at the gate heard one coming, he rang an alarm bell and we all tumbled out and watched it. As long as it's engine was running, it was no danger to us, but if the engine stopped we had to run for cover as it would descend rapidly and its 1000 lbs of explosive created quite a blast. All the while that we were in Valkenburg there were maybe three or four which landed close, none closer than one half mile, however. They made a great roar and left a huge crater but if you were three or four hundred yards away from the impact area you would be OK.

We slowly worked our way into Germany after Aachen was finally taken. We surveyed our way to the Roer River and watched as two towns, Julich and Duren, were bombed into oblivion. We wondered why the army didn't catch on to the fact that such bombing only created more hiding places for the German soldiers and actually prolonged the fight. We had the day off on Thanksgiving and our cooks, with the help of some of the former hotel cooks, outdid themselves. My mother preserved all of my letters and on 25 Nov., 1944, I wrote, "... We had our choice of white or dark turkey meat, so I had three large slices of white meat, two boiled potatoes, creamed peas, dressing, cranberry sauce, three baked rolls with fresh butter, and a fruit salad. There was enough for seconds on most everything, but the Army has cut down the appetite I used to have so I had all I could manage the first time. That meal really brought home to me the things I have to be thankful for; the outfit I'm in, the fact that I'm an American and that we are thought enough of to have the makings for a meal such as that shipped across the ocean to us. It takes a war to show a guy how much he has to be thankful for and to teach him not to be complacent or indifferent about so many of the little things that never seemed to matter before. I wish I could have shared that meal with some poor little kid over here, most of them have never in their lives seen anything like it and I used to take it all for granted!..." think it was absolutely the best meal I ever had while in the Army. Most of us became quite nostalgic, thinking of home A couple of weeks after that feast, our life of luxury ended. We moved to Kornelemunster, in Germany.

Hotel park Rooding, May, 1989

Germany

We took over an isolated brewery which had apparently been abandoned by the brewers not long before. The Brewery was located on a promontory above a vast quarry with cliffs on three sides of us and a chainlink fence, complete with a steel and barbed wire gate, on the landward side. Guarding the place was easy. We had one post at the gate and a roving post patrolling around the edge of the cliff. The buildings were never intended for living quarters, however. We lived in some storage rooms on the second floor. We went into the nearest town, broke down doors on houses that had no occupants and requisitioned stoves which we set up in the rooms we were occupying. The stove pipes went out through the window with one pane of glass broken out to make way for it. We were very rough on the Germans. No longer were we polite to civilians. We were ordered to take what we needed and our officers gave receipts, if they could find anyone to give them to, for the stoves, coal,etc. that we took. I always assumed that the receipts would be redeemed by the United States after the war, but I never heard if this was actually so.

We arrived here on the same day that the Battle of the Bulge started, December 16th. The first we heard of it was when our officers decreed greatly tightened security. There were rumors floating around about Germans in American uniforms so we were especially alert, and jittery, while on guard. I had guard duty at the gate, one bitter, cold night soon after the battle started. The temperature was well below zero, F. I had put on all the clothing that I could—long underwear, two pairs of pants, shirt, sweater, jacket, overcoat, two pairs of socks, boots, overshoes, a bath-towel over my head like an Arab with my helmet on over that. A pair of gloves under a pair of mittens completed my splendid attire. The only problem was that I couldn't move, and if I fell down I would never get up without assistance. I felt, and probably looked like, a giant teddy bear. But I was reasonably warm until the third hour of my four, and then I began to loose feeling in my feet and I couldn't hear too good because my teeth were chattering so loudly.

Nolan, that beautiful person, had the roving guard post and was supposed to exchange places with me periodically so that I could warm up by patrolling along the cliff and stopping in the kitchen for a minute or two for a cup of coffee. I hadn't seen him since sometime in the first hour. When the third hour passed with no sign of Nolan, I began to suspect foul play. He could have fallen off the cliff, but I doubted that I could be so lucky. It was more likely that he had holed up in the kitchen beside the stove and had gone to sleep. The gate was too far away from the buildings to get anyone's attention by shouting, and I was reluctant to fire my carbine which would wake everyone except Nolan, and as much as I disliked him, I didn't want to have him court-marshaled. So I paced back and forth like a tiger in a cage, 20 feet east, 20 feet west, back and forth, back and forth. The moon was nearly full in a cloudless sky and the night was brilliant with twinkling stars and millions of tiny reflections thrown off by the snow crystals, but the shadows were deeper and blacker than ever. I began to think that I was hallucinating when I realized the meteor which I was watching was going up, not down. I realized that I was probably observing one of Hitler's secret weapons, the V-2 rocket. How many miles away it was I have no idea, except that it was a long, long way off. I watched it rise, in a fish-tail path, until it disappeared directly overhead. There was no sound. Shortly after that I forgot all about the rocket or Nolan or the severe cold. There was someone walking toward me on the approach road.

I shifted my slung carbine to port-arms position and awaited his approach. He had on what appeared to be an American Officer's uniform so I expected that he was someone I might recognize. I halted him in the usual manner and asked for the password, which was changed everyday. His answer was unintelligible except for the fact that it sounded remarkably like German. I could feel the short hairs on my neck standing up like a scared dog's, and, pointing my carbine at him I asked for the password once more. It still sounded like German to me. I scanned the shadows on the road in back of him, half expecting to see a squad of German soldiers emerge, but there was no one there. In the slowly passing seconds while I was trying to make up my mind what to do, he started to reach under his coat, still speaking German. At that point I reacted swiftly by yelling very loudly at him in the few words of German that I knew, "Nicht. Nicht. Bewegen sie sich nicht. Hand Hoch. Hand der kopf." And I patted my helmet with my left hand. He knew by the tone of my voice that I was scared and that he was in very grave danger so he immediately locked his fingers on top of his head. I had exhausted my German vocabulary other than, "Raus mitt uns", but I didn't think that was appropriate, so I motioned for him to come through the gate and marched him into the company office. Capt. Kent was there with First Sgt. Leach and a couple of the lieutenants. They stared in amazement as this guy in Officer's uniform came through the door, with his hands on his head, with PFC Aldrich right behind him, pointing a loaded carbine at his back. It turned out that the officer was a Dutch liaison officer on official business. Everyone was too surprised to ask who was minding my post, which was fortunate, for I had abandoned it completely and the whole German army could have walked through the gate without firing a shot. I never did find out where Nolan was. Lt. "Wilkie" told me later that the Dutchman thought that I was going to kill him when he tried to reach under his coat for identification, and I told Lt. "Wilkie" that I had come within an inch of doing it. That was a very bad time to be walking around in an American uniform speaking what sounded like German.

At the height of the battle, the army was grabbing everyone who could point a rifle and pushing them in to plug the gaps. The engineers were fighting. The cooks and bakers of the infantry outfits were fighting, and green replacement troops with little or no training were being rushed to the front. I learned later that a kid two or three years younger than me, with whom I had gone to school, had been drafted, given nine weeks basic training, shipped to Europe with a replacement outfit, rushed to the front and killed in the Battle of the Bulge before anyone knew his name. Poor Herbie, he had been in the army less than twelve weeks. Anyway, one day we were ordered to line up in payroll order for interviews. The interviews, conducted by Capt. Kent and the other officers consisted of one question: "Can you think of any reason why you shouldn't be transferred to the Infantry?" There was such a chorus of wailing and lamenting that it would have made a good opera scene. There were bad backs, bad hips, bad feet, cases of tuberculosis, water on the knee, water on the brain, halitosis, blindness, athletes foot and rare ailments that no one had ever heard of. The married guys all had large families depending on them and even a couple of unmarried fellows claimed eleven or twelve kids. By the time my last-in-line turn came I was so disgusted that I answered, "No sir. I don't have any reason." All the officers burst out laughing. Lt. Wilkie said, "Well, at least we've got one honest man in the company." I don't think Capt. Kent intended to allow any of us to be transferred in any case, but he and the other officers surely did enjoy listening to all of that moaning and groaning.

The 19th Corp, to which we were attached was part of the 1st Army up until we got into Holland and then a paper transfer was made and all of the Corps in 1st Army became 9th Army. We were on the left flank of the American army with the British to our left, and the new 1st Army to our right. When Hitler's Ardennes offensive took place, 9th Army was, in effect, cut off from the rest of the Americans. For a week or so a few of us were moved to our left to work with the British and we were attached to them for rations and quarters. I liked the British soldiers, but couldn't stand the food. We had mutton, bully beef, bangers, char and bread which looked like mill sweepings—it probably was very nutritious, but we yearned for good old soft, white American bread. Fifty years later I probably would like that coarse British bread as I can't stand soft, white American bread. All rations became short and we had to go back to C rations for a while. Cigarettes disappeared completely and for awhile there they were worth their weight in gold. We were forbidden to fraternize with the Germans so our barter system had ended as soon as we crossed the boarder. We, that is, we band of brothers, managed to liberate some eggs and potatoes sometimes from some isolated farmers, being careful not to fraternize. One of our wags said that trading without conversation was not fraternization.

Tiger in the Forest

Winter had come on with a vengeance in December, '44. Bing Crosby's "I'll be home for Christmas" made the tears flow, but we already had plenty of snow. Our little group of surveyors set out one day to find a fire lookout tower in the Hurtgen Forest. We were going to set our theodolite up there and do some triangulation. The Hurtgen Forest was laid out with fire break lanes on a grid pattern. Having already picked out our route on a map, it seemed that it would be the easiest thing in the world to find it by counting roads. To begin with we only had one vehicle that day as our jeep was disabled for some reason or other. So six of us jammed into the weapons carrier and headed south from our brewery toward the battle. There was little or no traffic moving on the main road and the low gray clouds had began to lose their content of snow. We found what we assumed was the correct fire break trail and started into the forest.

We could hear the battle still going on in part of the forest some distance from us and every once in awhile we came upon places where heavy artillery fire had laid waste to relatively large areas. We came to a place where the trees had fallen over the road to such an extent that we had to detour. We backtracked to the next trail to our south and headed in that direction, counting trails to the east until we came to the one which should lead to the lookout tower. When we started into the forest there was about six inches of snow on the trails with no other vehicle tracks visible ahead of us. We stopped about noon time to eat and made a small fire under the trees to heat water for coffee, then went on with our search. The snow was accumulating at about an inch an hour so we were beginning to get somewhat anxious. We came to the block where the tower should have been but could find nothing so after an hour of fruitless circling about, Sgt Little decided that we should head back. He decided to take a short cut instead of following our search tracks but the trail he chose had deep ruts hidden by the snow and all four wheels dropped into them and turned like a kids toy with the tires about four inches from the bottom of the ruts. Fortunately no one had stolen the ax from its holder on the side of the truck so with it we cut a couple of 4" trees and used them as pry-bars to get the truck back onto solid ground where the wheels obtained traction and we were soon, once again on our way. We picked up our tracks a little further on, as Sgt Little said we would, and followed them back, although they were getting dim under the still falling snow and the failing light of late afternoon. Suddenly we came upon tank tracks in front of us, crossing our tracks. But these were no ordinary tank tracks, they were big, wide tracks which could only have been left by a German King Tiger. Not only that, but the tracks were fresh with no more than a dusting of snow on them. Other than our carbines, the biggest weapon that we had with us was the .30 cal. Machine-gun mounted on the windshield. Back at the company there were a couple of anti-tank bazookas, but even if we had them with us, they were no match for a Tiger. We six very frightened soldiers hauled out of there as fast as the driver dared to go on that rough track, expecting every minute to be hit by that tank's vicious 88. We got back to the brewery, cold, weary and too late for supper and had to eat cold C rations again. We didn't know at the time that we were heroes. Because of that day's outing the entire company got a battle star for the Ardennes battle. We never did go back looking for that fire lookout tower. We often wondered at the miracle of timing that kept us from meeting that fearsome German tank. None of us would have survived an encounter with that Tiger.

Winter into Spring

The Battle of the Bulge ended officially in late December, after the weather cleared enough for the planes to fly again. But it was mid January before the infantry was back at the same place where the battle had started. There were thousands of casualties on both sides, but Germany had used up her best and finest and everyone but Hitler knew that the war couldn't last much longer. There is a long gap in my letters home to Mom about here. I wrote on Dec. 16 and the next was Jan. 2. I never mentioned the battle to her nor Christmas either. Christmas was pretty bleak and although the Army again provided Turkey and fixings it wasn't much of a feast what with the cold and the battle going on within earshot of us. We tried some carol singing, but somehow "Silent Night, Holy Night..." didn't fit. I wondered how many more Christmases I would spend away from home. Would I ever spend another Christmas at home? Would there be another Christmas?

Alex Cardana, Charlie Smith and Roger working atop a slag heap at a coal mine in Germany.

We spent the rest of that cold and snowy January doing triangulation. As the Germans were slowly pushed back to the Rhine our travel time to our work sites became longer and longer. We were still quartered in the brewery which was now quite a ways back from the fighting, so we surveyors became commuters. My mother had worried about the long gap between letters and had contacted our Chaplain. He came to visit me one evening and we had a chat. He wrote Mom that he didn't get to visit the 62nd much because we were so far back from the front. This comforted Mom, but what he didn't tell her, and quite likely didn't know, was that our survey group spent more time close to the front than did the Combat Engineer group to which he was attached.

Sometime in early January, we were working from the top of a slag heap at a coal mine. Slag is waste rock taken from mines and this particular pile was a small mountain—maybe 300 feet high. We had to leave our vehicles about a half a mile away from the mine. We couldn't get them closer for there was an extensive German mine field blocking the route. We followed a narrow, zigzagging path that had been marked through the mines, being extremely careful not to step outside the marked, three foot wide path. Outside the taped safety zone there were twenty or thirty frozen bodies of American soldiers who had been killed when they stumbled into the mine field some days before. No one had time to clear the mines from the frozen ground, a dangerous task at best, so the bodies could not be retrieved. Although the distance across the mine field was only about one hundred yards, it usually took us about ten minutes of very careful walking to get from one side to the other. Once we were across we followed the access road to the mine complex and used a well-established trail up the slag pile to the summit where there was a small wooden building. The building was nothing more than a floor with posts to support the roof. It was intended as a shelter to keep the operator out of the elements. When the mine was in operation, there would be a person stationed in the building who controlled the chute that received the slag from a conveyor belt down at the mine head. At this time nothing was moving so we had the place all to ourselves. We set up our theodolite and turned angles all day, each day. With my issue binoculars I was supposed to scan the territory between us and the front line, about a mile and a half to two miles away, to make sure no one was sneaking up on us. With the binoculars I could get an occasional glimpse of German troops on the other side. It followed that if we could see them, they could see us if we got careless.

About the second or third day we all began to get jittery, what with the twice a day trip through the mine field and wondering if any Germans had noticed us working on the summit. As we went through the mine field that morning, I heard the corporal in front of me muttering something and I changed my focus from my feet to him. He said, "Morning, Joe. How're you today. Morning Charlie. Sleep well? Morning Jake. Not so cold this morning." I realized, with a start, that he was talking to the bodies on either side of us. We could clearly see their features, some with glassy, staring eyes, others turned away, all forever silent. Since they had frozen almost immediately after dying, they were not decomposing or bloating and day after day they looked as though they might wake up and go with us. I realized that there might be some who had not been killed by the mines, but being disabled to the point of not being able to move, had frozen to death. We were all getting very depressed. The usual joking and good natured banter stopped and we did our jobs zombie-like, with a minimum of talking to each other.

On the fourth morning, as we were going through the mine field, an artillery spotter plane buzzed us, flying very low. He did it not, once but several times. I suppose he thought we didn't know we were in a mine field and was trying to warn us. We were somewhat afraid that the vibrations he was setting up might touch off a mine so we waved him off and went so far as to point our weapons at him. He seemed to get the message and flew away. We were all, including Sgt. Little, very reluctant to go back up there on the fifth day, but Lt. Wilkie said that the plotters wanted another set of readings to insure accuracy. When we got through the mine field we stopped and had one more lengthy discussion about the necessity of climbing up the slag heap again. Lt. Wilkie was the only officer I ever knew who would allow discussions like that, and we all loved him for it. Someone voiced the opinion that we were really pressing our luck by going up there for a fifth day in a row. He had no more than got the words out when there was a tremendous series of explosions above us on the summit of the pile. We stood there, with our mouths open, in awe. When the dust and smoke cleared, we could see that the shack that we had worked out of had utterly disappeared. The Germans had hit the top of the pile with a "Time-on-Target". That is, maybe twenty or thirty guns, had been sighted on the slag pile and the time of flight of each gun's projectile figured so that they all arrived on the target at once. A mouse could not have lived on that summit. The only thing that had saved all of us was that our last discussion had resulted in delaying our usual time of arrival by about ten minutes. Silently, we picked up our burdens and went back through the mine field one last time. I think each of said a quiet good-bye to the bodies as we passed them. Once more we had been saved when others had died.

In one of my late January letters to Mom I mentioned going back to Valkenburg on a two-day pass. I stayed in the same hotel in which we had been bivouacked in November and December. The army had taken it over as a Rest and Recreation center. I told her that I slept a lot, went to a couple of movies, drank some warm beer and had an enjoyable two days away from the war. We could definitely sense that the war was winding down. We had more time off, there was not nearly the pressure we had worked under previously and we were all somewhat more relaxed. Whether this was good or bad for us, I have debated for a long time. When we worked at top speed with long hours, we didn't mind the primitive conditions or the lack of things to do for we were always so tired that we seldom could take advantage of any extra-curricular activities. When the pace slowed, we began to notice the utter boredom of our situation and actually looked forward to working closer to the enemy. There is a distinct possibility that we had become addicted to adrenaline.

We moved North from our brewery home about the first of February, when the weather started to warm up and we had rain instead of snow. We went to Munchen-Gladbach and took over a street (see photo below) where the Gestapo Chief owned all of the

buildings. We strung barbed wire at the entrance of the cul-de-sac and then went from house to house on both sides of the street, knocking on doors. Gulbenk, our German speaker told everyone that they had thirty minutes to pack up their belongings and leave. I tried to put myself in these peoples position. What would I take if ordered to leave my home in thirty minutes? There was no way that I could harden my heart against these people, most of whom were old. I could feel hate against Hitler and his gang. I could feel hate against the German people collectively for allowing the Nazis to start and continue all of this misery, but I found it impossible to hate these miserable, old people who were being turned out into the cold with nothing more than they could carry on their persons. We watched, with carbines at the ready, as they streamed from their homes, burdened with bundles, many of them weeping. The war was certainly coming home to them now. We moved into the vacated buildings and made ourselves as comfortable as possible. I don't think any of our people stole anything, but there was certainly a lot of rearrangement of stoves, beds, tables, chairs, etc. from one house to another. It must have taken those people a long time to sort out who owned what after we left. We found living conditions in these houses almost as bad as being out in the open. The roof leaked so badly in our bedroom that we set up our tents over our beds in order to keep them dry. We seemed to be constantly wet and there was no place to dry out. If we wanted to punish these Germans we should have left them to live in their own houses.

We were standing our morning Reveille and Roll Call one morning when we heard a very loud, thunderous noise which turned out to be a German plane with an engine pod on each wing but no propeller. The plane flew very fast and very low, maybe 500 ft., directly over us and then turned sharply up, as if trying to get back in the direction in which it came. Right behind the German were two American Lightening, P-38's, with guns blazing. At that low altitude the P-38's could out maneuver the German and they turned inside his turn and hit him with their fire and he exploded. We were astounded at all this. This was the first jet plane that we had ever seen, actually, we had never even heard of a jet plane. We found out later that the plane was a Messcherschmit 262, supposedly much faster than the Lightening, but they had jumped him as he was taking off and he was flying on the deck in an attempt to shake them off so that he could gain some altitude. Had he been able to do so, he could have easily left the P-38's behind.

While we were stationed here we did our last church steeple triangulation job. The church was out in the country and not in a town, but it was very close to a small river that was the dividing line between the American troops and the Germans. By very close I mean that the river was about a mile away. This brick church had been very much damaged by artillery fire and the front of the bell-tower was completely gone so that the steeple rested on the building and the two remaining sides of the tower. We had to climb rickety, old wooden ladders to get up into the belfry, and once there we had to scale up the internal beams of the steeple to reach a point where we could knock off tiles in a circle in order to see out all around and turn our angles. We laboriously carried planks up to lay them across the horizontal beams to make a platform to work on—nothing was nailed down and it was probably 35 to 40 feet down to the belfry floor. Below the belfry floor there was nothing but ladders for about 100 feet down to the ground, for the other three floors had fallen with the front wall.. The artillery people sent an observer up with us. He was directing fire on the German positions on the other side of the small river, using a periscopic range finder. I watched, through my binoculars, the same scene that he watched, while the rest of our crew turned angles for triangulation. On the other side of the stream there were a lot of high bushes which, the artillery spotter said, probably concealed a German strong-point. We watched as a German army ambulance came over the crest of the hill and disappeared behind the bushes. Soon it reappeared going back up and over the ridge and out of sight. We watched what appeared to be the same ambulance, make about five round trips and the artilleryman told me he thought they were carrying troops in rather than taking wounded out. He called in for some ranging shots on the slope of the ridge about one hundred yards away from the track that the ambulance was using and then told the battery that he was working with to shift their aiming point one hundred yards to the left, load with white phosphorous shell and wait. The ambulance appeared once more and as it started to descend the grade the spotter yelled, "Fire", into his phone. Seconds later the area around the ambulance fountained with deadly, burning white phosphorous, the ambulance burst into flame and out of the rear burst about ten German infantrymen, running for dear life. The spotter then shifted target to the bushes on the river's edge and called in a barrage of HE (High Explosive). When the barrage stopped we could see German infantry retreating up over the ridge.

A group of American P-47's appeared on the scene and started to dive-bomb a position in back of the ridge out of our sight. The were met with bursts of anti-aircraft fire and one of the planes was hit. Smoke began streaming from the P-47's engine and he turned and wobbled back toward us. He was obviously not going to get far and just as he came overhead, the pilot bailed out. The pilot-less plane nosed over and started down in a power dive, with it's engine howling and it looked to us as though the plane was lined up straight for the church we were in. We watched the plane come at us with much the same fascination that a mouse has while waiting for a snake to strike. There was no time to make the lengthy descent on the ladders and no place to hide. I am sure that each of us came to the same conclusion in those few seconds while the plane screamed down toward us. Fate had caught us at last. We were going to die. We could actually see the heavy bombs on each of the wings and we knew with absolute certainty that they would explode on contact. The P-47 missed our church by about one hundred and fifty yards and exploded in an open field with a huge flash and roar and a cloud of black smoke and dirt. The church tower rocked back and forth as if a giant were shaking it---tiles fell off the steeple roof, bricks fell from where they had been loosened and further back in the church part of the roof fell in with a roar almost as loud as the exploding plane. We each grabbed on to any beam within reach, as our theodolite toppled and went over the edge of the platform. A lot of dust, old pigeon droppings and pieces of the steeple roof rained down on us and a few of the loose planks that made up our platform went fluttering down like leaves. As the dust settled we looked out to see a huge crater, with a small fire flickering on what looked like the engine—all that was left of the plane. Drifting down to land beside the crater was the pilot.

We scrambled cautiously down the ladders and Lt. Wilkie ran down to the pilot to see if he was all right. Other than being shaken up, the pilot was OK and Lt. Wilkie told him he was probably not half as shaken or scared as we were. When we got back to our bivouac area, late that February afternoon, everyone else had started to eat supper. We tried our best to ignore the usual banter, such as, "Where have you guys been goofing off all day while us poor slaves have been doing your work and ours too?" I found myself coming down off an adrenaline high, and too emotionally drained to answer any questions like, "How was your day?" I gave noncommittal grunts and went off to be alone with my mess kit full of food which I only picked at. My stomach was still tied up in knots and all I could manage to get down was a cup of iodine-tasting black coffee. We never had to do another steeple job, which was just as well, for there would probably have been a mutiny. We had all had enough of steeples to last us a lifetime.

As February became March and March became April we found the battle moving further and further away from us and our work. The Rhine crossing at Remagen was the beginning of the race to the end of the war in Europe. The Ninth Army and the British made assault crossings to the North and once the East bank was secure we moved across the river. We once did some coordinate work for the artillery at a place where they had an 8 inch rifle sited. An eight inch rifle was about the same gun as the Navy's heavy cruisers used. The artillerists were firing at targets about 18 to 20 miles away and they needed an accurate survey. I got a kick out of watching the fire procedure of that huge gun. The gun crew trundled the shell up to the gun and rammed it into the tube with a heavy rammer. Next came powder bags in increments calculated to give the shell a kick hard enough to enable it to reach the target. On the command to fire one of the crew yanked a lanyard and the gun roared. There was a sheet of flame that belched out in front of the gun for what seemed like a hundred to one hundred fifty feet and set the dry grass afire. They had two men with wet gunny-sacks, stationed in front and to each side. It was their job to beat out the grass fire each time the gun fired. I mentioned to Lt. "Wilkie" that I would like to pull the lanyard to fire that gun. A little while later I saw him talking to the lieutenant in charge of the gun and they came walking over to where I was standing. The artillerist told me that I could fire the next shot if I wanted, so I got to pull the lanyard. I never did know what they were firing at, so I don't know what, if anything, I hit. I found that I could live with myself better if I didn't have to know if I had killed anyone.

Rhineland

Across the Rhine, while the 9th and 1st Armies were encircling the Rhur pocket we found ourselves with little to do other than mark time. We spent a great deal of time looking for possible triangulation points and exploring the countryside. We came upon an abandoned German army post one day. The gates were padlocked but we easily broke them and went in to find that the facility was a supply depot. We found clothing, uniforms, helmets, canvas equipment, but no weapons. We broke into one warehouse and were stunned to find food in abundance while outside there were people starving. We found large cans of meat stew by the crate, we found crates of canned Portuguese sardines and we found large, wicker-covered demijohns of cognac—truckloads of the stuff. Lt. Wilkie decided that he had better go back to the outfit and report all of this. He left three of us there to guard the post and keep everyone out if possible. We realized that he couldn't possibly be back for two or three hours so we decided that we had better have some refreshments. We opened a can of the meat stew and heated it on a little fire of refuse outside on the cobblestones. It was really good stuff, far better than the C rations we were supposed to be eating. It tasted like a beef stew so we decided that's what it must be. We had sardines for desert. Could it be that the German army was eating better than we were? We heated water for coffee and then decided that a little cognac in the coffee wouldn't be bad. It wasn't. As a matter of fact it was delicious but it was a bad idea. We had, finally, found an additive that made iodized water and powdered coffee palatable. From the American Heritage Dictionary: "Palatable—Agreeable to the taste. Acceptable to the mind or sensibilities." Yes, it was all of the above. We had another cup. We ate some more stew. We had more coffee-con-cognac. We went and got some German helmets and did some goose-step marching and Heil-Hitlering. We had more coffee.

By the time Lt. "Wilkie" got back, accompanied by three two-and-a-half ton trucks, we were ready to dance but we couldn't find any girls. Lt. Wilkie ordered us into the weapons carrier and told us to keep still. As a matter of fact, what he said was, "You guys get in the truck and keep your damned mouths shut and I mean, don't talk to anyone, and just maybe I won't have to have you court-martialed." The rest of the men loaded one truck with the meat stew and sardines and the other two with all the five gallon demi-johns of cognac that they could manage, including one, which had been opened and was mysteriously missing about a quart. By that time, other trucks from other 19th Corp units were arriving, for Capt. Kent had called in the location of the booty after giving Lt. Wilkie about a two hour head start. The next morning, Capt. Kent told the assembled company what we had found the previous day. He said that our German speaker, Gulbenk, had informed him that the labels on the cans of meat stew said that the content was horse meat, but since it had already been tested on three unnamed individuals, and they had survived, the company cooks were authorized to use it and those who didn't want to eat it could stick with their own C rations. The sardines would be passed out each day to those who wanted them and the cognac would be rationed out each evening at supper time a la Brit Navy.

That was the plan. It didn't quite work out that way. About one third of the company began showing up at morning roll call in a less than sober state. It took a few days for the officers to discover that the men were forming groups of three or four and one of them would be the designated celebrant of the evening, with the others donating their ration to him. New rule coming up. Everyone had to show an empty canteen cup upon leaving the mess area. That didn't work either. The canteen cups were emptied into the canteens. Next rule: NO CANTEENS IN THE MESS AREA. Beer bottles appeared on the scene. They could be concealed under the jacket, in the waist band of the trousers. We were at a point where there wasn't nearly so much work for us and we were slowing down on weekends, so Capt. Kent called an assembly for noon on Friday. He said that we had to get rid of the cognac, as The Corp. Headquarters Officers who were visiting us had begun to be suspicious of the happy attitude of the people in the 62nd. He declared a weekend off—no kitchen duties, only one guard at the entrance, (we were quartered in an old School building formerly occupied by the Hitler Youth movement), but no weekend passes. Everyone was confined to the area. He further said that any Cognac left at 5 am Monday would be dumped down the latrine. Quite a few officers from Corp. Headquarters arrived to help with this clean-up operation. Capt. Kent needn't have worried, there was no Cognac left to dump on Monday.

I often wondered how many of those people became alchoholics after the war. Liquor was available at any time and many guys seemed never to be quite sober. We had a Medical Corp Corporal attached to our company - he was our "doctor"- and he was the main "bootlegger." He had a bottomless supply of medicinal alcohol in one gallon cans. This potent, 200 proof liquid, when mixed in a canteen cup with an equal amount of highly acidic, canned grapefruit juice would separate ones head from ones shoulders and burn a hole in ones stomach about five feet deep. Drugs were not a problem in WW II. Alcohol was.

Our guys ran the gamut from happy drunks to mean drunks, from sleepy drunks to "lets have a party" drunks. I got caught by a couple of the mean drunks one night. I was on guard duty when they came stumbling around looking for something to eat from the kitchen truck. I made the mistake of trying to quiet them down for fear that the officers would wake up. One of them was a big one. He grabbed my carbine away from me, threw it about 40 feet away, grabbed me by the shoulders and slammed me up against the brick wall of the house, right under the Captain's window. My helmet came down over my eyes and my boots weren't touching the ground. I decided that they could take all the bread they wanted - take the truck too - eat it for desert. Watch out for those mean drunks.

Schloss von Metternich

On the 10th of April, we arrived at a place in Germany called
Visenbeck and made quite a sight as our convoy of muddy,
war-weary vehicles drove through the gates of a magnificent
chateau, and down the circular drive to park on the manicured
grounds of the owner, Count Wolf von Metternich.

It was obvious that some evil genius at Corp Headquarters had a
hate for German officialdom. I well remember seeing the Count, a
silver-haired, very erect, old Prussian type coming down the ornate
staircase from the castle entrance and pouring out a torrent of
German at Capt. Kent. Gulbenk translated for Capt. Kent and
informed the Count that we were to be his guests for a few days.

The officers looked over the castle interior and informed us that the everyone below rank of Master Sergeant was to bed down in the drawing room. The drawing room was huge, light and airy with floor to ceiling windows, highly polished floors and antique, delicate furniture. We moved in, piled all the furniture in one corner of the room, rolled up the carpets and spread out our bed-rolls. After supper, which we ate outside in the warm spring air, the technical people filled our water wagon from a stream that was fed by a pond and discovered that the pond was teeming with very large brown trout. Early the next morning someone decided to try his luck and easily caught a big hungry one with some twine and a bent-pin fishhook. Within minutes the banks of the pond were crowded with anglers. Frying pans appeared, appropriated from the chateau kitchen, and little smoky fires burst out by magic and teams were formed, one fisherman, one food-prep technician (fish-gutter), and one cook. Fresh fish! The first fresh fish since leaving home, years ago. The Count appeared shouting and cursing and one of the sergeants told him, through Gulbenk, to shut up, and get back in the castle before he was shot for interfering with the United States Army. He went to find Capt. Kent who told him to submit a bill to higher headquarters when he found time. Somewhere, among my few wartime souvenirs, I have one of Count Wolf von Metternich's cards. We moved on after a pleasant four-day interlude at Schloss Metternich. It was time to go back to war anyway as there were no more trout in that pond.

We began to see thousands of German prisoners walking West along the median strip of the Autobahn while American vehicles of all kinds went East on both travel lanes. There would only be one or two Americans guarding hundreds of prisoners. When the resistance in the Ruhr pocket collapsed, there were so many prisoners that the army was hard-pressed to take care of them all. We learned later that there had been a very real danger that a disaster would develop, for it became next to impossible to feed and house this mass of humanity. Conditions in the hastily improvised prison camps soon approached those of an Andersonville, but the army mounted a gigantic effort and solved the problem before it became a national disgrace.

In mid April, we did, what turned out to be our last high triangulation job. We were to work from the top of a very high water storage tower. I don't know where we were except that the tower was a little way off a paved highway on a very flat plain somewhere East of the Rhur. We had driven through Hamlin about that time. I was intrigued by wondering if the rats or the children would follow us.

The first morning that we worked at the site there was such a thick fog that we couldn't see the top of the tower. The tower was surrounded by a sugar beet field and off in the distance we could see some animals grazing. Someone said, "Look at the horses grazing out there." I said, "No, they can't be horses, look at the long ears, they must be mules." About that time the fog started to lift and what we had taken to be horses or mules, 300 or 400 yards away, turned into rabbits less than a 100 feet away. Very embarrassing, and showing that by calling a rabbit a mule one could make an ass of one's self.

Once the fog had lifted we started to carry our equipment up to the top of the tower. The base was a round brick structure about 100 feet high and maybe 100 feet in diameter. On the inside wall of this cylinder there was a staircase with railing spiraling up to the top in one turn, so that the top of the stairs were directly over the bottom. There were windows at intervals along the stairs so that the interior of the cylinder was lighted naturally. From the top of the stairs there was a flying bridge which joined a staircase which spiraled up into the center of the tank. I have no idea how tall the tank was. Maybe 100 feet, maybe 75, certainly not less than 60. The electricity wasn't working so the spiral staircase had to be navigated in total, absolute darkness, unless one was a Sgt. or a Lieutenant and had command of a flashlight. I had never had any fear of heights, but I must admit that crossing that 45 feet of flying bridge, about 100 feet off the floor, made my knees tremble. But the bridge didn't hold a candle to the claustrophobia I felt once I had made one complete turn up that spiral staircase and all light disappeared. Every time I had to ascend or descend those stairs I became completely disoriented. I tried counting stairs but my irrational fears always got the best of me and I always lost count. I was always amazed to find that eventually I would come to the top or bottom, depending upon which way I was going. I was always just on the knife edge of panic as I reached the light and I wondered what would happen if I had to negotiate another 20 feet of spiral.

I realized that the phobia, which had first manifested itself so long ago, was growing inside me and I wondered how much longer I would be able to keep it bottled up; how much longer would I be able to keep it hidden from my companions. The only time that I had not been able to control this phobia was way back at Camp Edwards. I think I mentioned that the lines for meals were monstrous, stretching for a half a mile or so, four abreast. I had gotten on the tail of the line one day, the outside person on the left of the line. The mess hall was a huge building which may have been a hanger for all I know. As the line inched forward I found myself on the inside of the line, with the building on my left and three men on my right. Somewhere far to the rear, people started pushing forward and when this force reached us we were squeezed as in a giant vise. I couldn't breathe, and I couldn't move and I could feel the panic rising. I asked the people beside me to let me out. They laughed at me and I asked again, more urgently this time. Again they laughed. Panic took over completely and I exploded. I took off my helmet and started swinging it like a club with a strength that I never had before. I took a wedge of men beside me, in front of me and behind me out of the line amid name calling and dire threats. I think that if those men hadn't been completely awed by my panic-induced strength, they would have beaten me up, as it was I simply walked to the rear of the line and got on the right side of it this time. Knowing that it could happen, I was in constant fear that it would happen again.

The roof of the reservoir gently sloped downward from the center and was surrounded by a waist-high parapet. The diameter of the tank was so much greater than the base that we could not see the base even when leaning out over the parapet. We had to measure the height of the tower with a measuring wire with plumb bob attached. We didn't know when we finished there that that was our last triangulation job of the war.

Roger eating cold baked beans straight out of the can. They were a present from home. We were in convoy again, somewhere East of the Rhine.

The River Elbe

We arrived at a town called Oschersleben on the 14th of April, '45. Oschersleben is about 15 miles west of Magdeburg, on the Elbe River. Magdeburg is 75 to 80 miles from Berlin. We ran our survey into Magdeburg and down to the edge of the River. We watched as a group of Combat Engineers pushed a pontoon foot bridge across the river and that was where the war ended for us. We watched the Russians arrive on the East bank—so much horse drawn equipment, it was a wonder they ever got anywhere. We shook hands with a few of them who came over the foot-bridge and then we had orders to move camp back to Goslar which is in the Hartz Mountains. Goslar was just a kilometer or so inside what was to become the American Zone and the border between East and West Germany, the boundary had already been set at Yalta. I have often seen criticism of General Eisenhower for not taking Berlin, but I never have been able to understand why the critics think the push should have been made. The political boundaries had been decided upon long before and, with the war all but over, what was the point in taking territory simply to give it to the Soviets. Did we really need all that chest beating? After all, Berlin was only a symbol. The only result would have been more US lives lost uselessly.

We were in Goslar on May 7. We were awakened sometime in the early morning, before daylight, by weapons firing wildly. We all got up, grabbed our weapons and prepared to defend our perimeter, but we were told that some adjoining unit had just learned that Germany had surrendered and they were celebrating by firing their weapons wildly into the sky. The War was over. Some of the guys decided to stay up an talk until daylight but I went outside and sat under a tree by myself. I didn't want to talk to anyone. I thought about all the dead soldiers I had seen in the eleven months since we had landed on Omaha Beach. I remembered the last one, back near the Rhine. He was lying with his face in the mud, both hands under him, clutching his rifle. He was dead before he hit the ground for he never tried to break his fall. If only he could have made it for another couple of weeks. Was he a veteran?

Was he a new replacement? Did his family know yet that he was dead? Was it possible that he was the last man to die here in this German mud? Had his death served any useful purpose? Had I served any useful purpose? Was there meaning to all this horror, this madness, that had taken three years out of my life? I felt depressed when I should have felt elated, but I didn't know why. I remembered a passage in a book I had obtained from the Army Special Services, shortly before. The Duke of Wellington, had written in a dispatch after the Battle of Waterloo, "Nothing except a battle lost can be half so melancholy as a battle won."

Garrison duty in Butzbach

My next letter home to Mom is dated 15 May, 1945. I don't know why I waited so long to write, but since I sounded severely depressed in my letter, I probably just wanted to be alone and talk or write to no one. President Roosevelt's death, coming shortly before, had a bad effect on our morale. At the same time I had received a "Dear John" letter from my girl friend; she had fallen in love with a classmate in college and they were getting married right after they graduated in June. To add to all of this we had moved from Goslar and were in a semi-permanent garrison in Butzbach.

On the day we were to move Capt. Kent had said that if any of us wished he would let one truck go to Butzbach by way of Buchenwald so that we could see first hand what the Germans had done to the Jews. Eight or ten of us chose to go, including the two Jewish boys in the Company. I have never been able to talk about that experience. Many times when people would ask if I had gone to see a concentration camp, I would lie and say, "No, I never did." I couldn't bear to describe it. I tried to suppress those awful sights and smells; I tried desperately to erase it all from my memory, but I couldn't. My only escape was to deny that I had been there. To this day, I can't talk or write about it. Do not ask me to say more for I will not. Suffice it to say that everything you have ever read about those camps is true, but not everything was written about. All of the photographs you have seen are true representations, but some things were never photographed. For those of you who were not there, be thankful to your God that you were not.

My May 15th letter:

Dear Mom & Dad, Well, V-Day came and went and was just another day for us. Most of us aren't quite sure yet just which day it was. There was no celebration, no cheering, no parades or confetti. No girls to kiss, no drums or bugles, no bands playing. There was just an attitude of, "Well, that's over, now what's next?" As you know, the point system for demobilization has been announced, but as far as I am concerned it doesn't matter much. I have just about enough points to enable me to get a free trip to the Pacific for 2 or 3 years. But don't worry about it, for I'm going to get through this thing no matter how many years it takes. We have moved again and are now quartered in a former German Army Officers Candidate School. It is a pretty nice place and we aren't very crowded. There are three of us in our room. We have showers with Hot and Cold water and a large kitchen and mess hall.

The weather has decided to come summer and where we had been chilly, we are now sweltering with hot, sunny days. I bet the kids in school are getting ready for summer now, huh? I can remember how I used to look forward to it. The seasons don't make much difference now. I suppose it was the fact of looking forward to vacation the made the summer seem so pleasant. Now there is no vacation, not even for a week, so spring summer, fall and winter just come and go. Sometimes I get so tired of it all, I'd like to get

80

away somewhere by myself and just do as I please. Do you remember the last time I was home? I have had exactly four days of leave since then. Two days in London and two in Valkenburg, Holland. We can't talk to the German's because of the non-fraternizing policy, but I'd sure like to have a conversation with someone besides a GI once in awhile. We get to see 2nd or 3rd rate movies, the USO shows are few and far between, and we get a visit from the Redcross Donut-mobile maybe once in two months and then the girls don't talk to enlisted men--just to officers. Fortunately, we get a very good selection of paper-back books from Special Services and books keep me going .... This part of the war is over but what comes next, no one knows. The only thing to do is wait and see. We will probably find out soon enough. Don't build up any hopes about my coming home though, for it is going to be a long time and I may come home by way of the Pacific.

Love to you all, Rog

It quickly became obvious that we were going to stay in Butzbach for a long time and we nervously settled into a garrison routine. I say nervously for we all found it very difficult to make the abrupt transition from black-outs to lights. We had lived in a fight-or-flight situation for so long that we no longer knew what was

81

normal—war or peace? I wrote, "—we see German soldiers coming home now. They remind me of pictures in history books of southern Civil War soldiers coming home. They are bedraggled and ragged and have a beaten look. Not a superman to a carload and I've yet to see one look arrogant.." At the time that I wrote that letter, 24 May, about a dozen men of the company had already left for the States and discharge. Moving the top ranks out made room for those of us on the bottom to advance and I was already a tech-corporal. In the next letter, written on 1, June, I told my Mom that more of our company men had gone home and that I had now been advanced to Corporal which meant that I would have no more Guard Duty or KP. By the 9th of June I wrote that I was taking over the Supply Room and was being advanced to sergeant as fast as possible. The Army was obviously going to retain our Topographic Engineer unit and since we were of no further use here in Europe the reason for our retention became clear. We would be needed if a Japanese invasion was planned.

The Old Timers left rapidly as their point totals came to the top of the list. First Sgt. Leach left and one of the fellows who came over on the same troopship with me, Bill Pierce, took over the Headquarters Platoon as acting First Sergeant while I became acting Supply Sgt. Our rank did not catch up with us till later as there was some silly regulation about promotions—one grade per month—or something like that. By July, I was a full blown, dyed-in-the-wool, Old Timer with the. Rank of Sergeant and could bark with authority at the green new replacements we were getting. Garrison duty was dull and routine and terribly boring. We were, of course, full of anxiety about whether or not we were going to Japan. In late July things began to move. We had orders to start turning in all of our equipment as rapidly as possible. This meant that the Army was gambling that either we wouldn't be needed in Japan, or if needed we would be issued new equipment somewhere on the way. Since I had been appointed the new Supply Sgt. it became my duty to account for, and turn in all of the equipment—press trucks, photo-mapping equipment, theodolites, calculators, binoculars, ammunition, weapons, tents, mess equipment—a thousand and one pieces of hardware. Everything had to be checked against the list of equipment we were supposed to have. Soldiers being the acquisitive creatures that they are, I never came up short, but had the headache of having to cover up the very large surplus of items that we had, many that we were not even supposed to know about. Since I had been a lowly PFC until after V-E day, I hadn't the slightest idea where all this stuff had come from. The Lieutenant in charge of Supply was a new replacement and knew even less about all of this than I did. He and I used to share the duty of riding shotgun on the convoys to the supply depots where we had to turn in the stuff and get signed receipts to show that we had properly done so. Some of these runs took us two and three days and, as NCO in charge, I had to obtain rations and quarters for the drivers and myself if we had to be away overnight. I was stunned at the waste and inefficiency of the Army's abandonment of its material in it's haste to get everyone out of the service as soon as possible. I have often wondered what happened to all of that stuff. There were hundreds of acres of vehicles of every kind parked bumper to bumper, out in muddy, open fields. We dumped all of our optical equipment in a huge pile of similar equipment from other outfits. No cover at all—left there to rot.

There were welcome breaks in this routine. We went to Heidelburg on July 29, to see Dinah Shore in a USO performance, and had time to explore the old part of the city and the Castle. Our closest leave city was Bad Neuheim and we went there frequently. We went to a circus once in early July. The circus, owned by an Englishman, had been stranded in Czechoslovakia or somewhere and was slowly working its way home to England, paying its way by performances along the road. I sat next to a Colonel and had a great conversation with him, about the circus, the performers, the war, the United States, college and life in general. The circus was fun, but the conversation was even better. In August, I wrote about seeing Bob Hope and Ingrid Bergman and also about being promoted to Staff Sergeant and compensated by the princely sum of $110.00 per month. The BOMB was dropped on 10 August and the second one soon thereafter. I wrote about the end of the war—again we had no celebration—just a sadness.

Closing Down My War

After everything had been turned in, I was given a one week furlough and had a choice of the Riveria or Switzerland. The price of the week was $35.00, cash and we were allowed to take $35.00 with us. I had to borrow $50.00 from a buddy to be able to go. I chose Switzerland and had a wonderful time. The Swiss, who had been neutral all during the war, had no hesitation in showing where their sympathies lay and treated us like royalty.

I have a picture taken in Bern, of me sitting on a park bench with a very beautiful girl. In the picture I look worried but the girl looks delighted, sort of like a fisherman showing off the catch of the day. She spoke excellent English and I enjoyed the day, my first day of female companionship since I had been to London to see Mary almost a year and a half before. That girl never will grow old. She will always be young and beautiful and exciting and fifty years later I can still hear her giggle. I wonder what her name was?

Roger and friends from another unit, in Switzerland

When I got back to Butzbach the outfit had been broken up in my absence. There were only fifteen people left and we were transferred to a Combat Engineer Battalion for transportation back to the states. I never got a chance to say good-bye to most of the people with whom I had shared fright, laughter, sorrow, joy, heat, cold, dust, mud, life and death. I never said good-bye to Lt. Wilkinson (Wilkie). It was probably just as well. I would never have been able to control my emotions. I've not mentioned it before, but an outfit, a unit, like our small Company, is a soldiers home; it is his family and, in a war like World War II, soldiers

85

would go to great lengths to get back to their company if separated. I once refused hospitalization for a skin condition for fear that I wouldn't be able to catch up. While we might get sick of each other and fight and call each other names we would defend to the death any member of the company against any number of "others." Our little band of surveyors had looked death in the face together many times, a bond that comes to very few people. While many people may have had close encounters with death, it must be very rare for a small group of people to share multiple encounters with death. I had very mixed emotions about saying good-bye in those far off days. Isn't it sad that we have to live so many lifetimes before we know how to live. A favorite quote from one of my favorite authors, Richard Bach, *"Don't be dismayed at good-byes. A farewell is necessary before you can meet again. And meeting again, after moments or lifetimes, is certain for those who are friends."*

Omega

We went to a holding camp in France, just outside of Le Havre, around 1 Sept., and marked time there until early October. I wrote that there was nothing to do except sleep and read. I wrote that I didn't go to movies any more as they were so crowded that my "claustrophobia" got the better of me. I said that I had thought that I would be getting over it and was surprised that it seemed to be getting worse. Little did I realize that it would be forty years before I would "get over it." Nor did I have any idea that my phobia was not claustrophobia, but an offshoot of agora-phobia, a fear of being afraid—a fear of showing fear—a terrible thing in the eyes of a soldier. So I came home with an unrecognized, severe case of post-traumatic stress—a phrase that has only been coined since the Viet Nam conflict. Am I cured? No. But that old phobia is certainly in an arrested state, since, with the aid of a couple of books and a lot of self analysis, I have come to recognize it for what it is.

Finally, in early October, we were loaded onto a troop ship and headed West. The return trip was vastly different than the War time voyage of December, '43. Since I was a Staff Sergeant I rated a state room—shared with four other sergeants. There were only two beds and they would accommodate only two per bed, so as ranking sergeant, I chose to sleep in the bath tub on the barrack bags piled in it. We had another stormy, but otherwise uneventful crossing, docked in Boston and were sent to Camp Edwards for processing. I had come full circle. I had returned to the place of beginning. Three years and fourteen days after I had enlisted, I was out. It was finished ~ ~ ~

Epilogue

But.....it was not finished. It was always there, just under the surface, like a land mine waiting, waiting, waiting. I would wake up at night, drenched with sweat and with a sense of terror. Nancy would ask me if I was all right and I would say, "Yes, it's nothing, I'm OK," and then I would lie awake and stare at the inside of my eyelids. Every single one of those young, dead soldiers went by like a slide show, like they were passing in review --- all of them—again and again and again. I had monstrous guilt feelings. What did my three years of service accomplish? Did I save even one person's life? Did my personal contribution shorten the war by even one minute? Why did I survive when so many, many others had been killed? Why had I not been wounded when so many others were maimed for life? I didn't recognize the fact that I had indeed been wounded, and severely wounded at that. A wound that would take forty years to heal.

In 1985, forty-one years after first going to Normandy, my Mom, my sister Nancy, my wife Nancy and I went with a tour group to France and Switzerland. While we were in Paris we rented a car and drove out to Normandy and Omaha Beach. It was springtime and everything was green and beautiful. It was just a few weeks short of the forty first anniversary of my landing there on 22 June 1944. I left the others and walked alone ~ ~ ~

As I walked on that immense, empty stretch of sand I wondered if I could be walking on the same tiny grains of sand that I had walked on so long before. How long does it take for a grain of sand to disappear? Were they still there, those grains of sand from so many years ago?

The Ships were gone. In June of 1944 it seemed like there were hundreds of them. Some were at anchor, off the beach, waiting their turn to unload. Many had their bows up on the beach with their cavernous mouths open, disgorging men and tanks and jeeps and guns and trucks full of rations, ammunition and equipment. Those ships, LST's, sat there, shoulder to shoulder for as far as I could see They are gone now. The beach is empty

As I stood there, alone, I remembered the men. They were there in thousands. In trucks, bulldozers, jeeps and weapons carriers and tanks. There were men coming ashore, wading up to their chests in the cold, cold surf. There were men running on the hard sand and forming up by platoons and companies to move up through the beach exits toward the sound of the guns. There were dead men there too. They were bloated and misshapen and grotesque and I felt anger toward them for being there among the living and for having waited so long to be buried.

And then there was the noise. An incredible cacophony of pounding, roaring surf, of clanking, shrieking machinery, of sergeant's whistles, of ship's guns firing, of shells whooshing overhead. Of explosions, of strafing machine guns from one lone German FW 190, and the incongruous sound of laughter caused by the ever-present, raucously humorous bravado of frightened men. Except for the sound of the sea crashing on the shore and the mournful cry of the gulls the noise is gone now. There is silence. Waiting, watchful silence.

There are still few crumbling pillboxes above the tide line, with their rusty cannons forever silent, inside. There is a gigantic box-shaped piece of concrete resting on the beach at a crazy angle. It was a part of the floating docks of an artificial harbor that broke up and came ashore in the tremendous storm of 19, June. I first set foot on that beach on the day after the concrete box stranded there. The box is now the shore end of a fishing pier. The beach goers pay no attention to what it is or was. To them it is nothing more than a broken relic of some long gone people. But I know what it is. I survived the storm that killed it and left it there to weather away into eternity.

High up on the bluff overlooking the beach is a cemetery. The grounds are manicured, the grass is green, the flowers are forever beautiful and there are tall, solemn monuments of stone with all the right words carved into them. And then there are the crosses. The crosses and the Stars of David. No matter where one stands, no matter where one looks the crosses stretch away in straight lines, seemingly to infinity.

All the rows of crosses converged at the point where I stood and all of the crosses silently asked, "Why are you here?" My whispered answer was, "I survived the fire storm that killed all of you and I wanted to see you once more." Oh yes, I saw them there before. Heaped in piles on the beach, awaiting burial. I saw them where they had been violently flung, like rag dolls, in the fields and on the hedgerows. I saw them in the ditches of the long, dusty road to St. Lo and I saw them churned to bits in the rubble of that terrible place. I saw them, oh Dear God, yes, I saw them.

But now they were gone. Only the crosses and the Stars of David and the sand and the sea and the sky were left. I had an immense feeling of release—a weight had been lifted from me. I was at peace. My ghosts were gone. Those old ghosts that had been with me for all those years. They had slipped away into the sea, washed there by my tears as I stood once more on the sand of that beach in Normandy called "Omaha."

   ~ ~ ~now, at last, it was finished.